# Latin America

*Studies in International Economics*

# Latin America
## The Crisis
## of Debt and Growth

*Thomas O. Enders and Richard P. Mattione*

THE BROOKINGS INSTITUTION
*Washington, D.C.*

THE BROOKINGS INSTITUTION is an independent organization devoted to nonpartisan research, education, and publication in economics, government, foreign policy, and the social sciences generally. Its principal purposes are to aid in the development of sound public policies and to promote public understanding of issues of national importance.

The Institution was founded on December 8, 1927, to merge the activities of the Institute for Government Research, founded in 1916, the Institute of Economics, founded in 1922, and the Robert Brookings Graduate School of Economics and Government, founded in 1924.

The Board of Trustees is responsible for the general administration of the Institution, while the immediate direction of the policies, program, and staff is vested in the President, assisted by an advisory committee of the officers and staff. The by-laws of the Institution state: "It is the function of the Trustees to make possible the conduct of scientific research, and publication, under the most favorable conditions, and to safeguard the independence of the research staff in the pursuit of their studies and in the publication of the results of such studies. It is not a part of their function to determine, control, or influence the conduct of particular investigations or the conclusions reached."

The President bears final responsibility for the decision to publish a manuscript as a Brookings book. In reaching his judgment on the competence, accuracy, and objectivity of each study, the President is advised by the director of the appropriate research program and weighs the views of a panel of expert outside readers who report to him in confidence on the quality of the work. Publication of a work signifies that it is deemed a competent treatment worthy of public consideration but does not imply endorsement of conclusions or recommendations.

The Institution maintains its position of neutrality on issues of public policy in order to safeguard the intellectual freedom of the staff. Hence interpretations or conclusions in Brookings publications should be understood to be solely those of the authors and should not be attributed to the Institution, to its trustees, officers, or other staff members, or to the organizations that support its research.

134946

# Foreword

DURING the last two years, most Latin American nations have been forced to reschedule large amounts of bank loans and to seek assistance from the International Monetary Fund. This debt crisis has greatly concerned Western bankers and government officials because of the sheer magnitude of the loans outstanding. Latin Americans, on the other hand, have described the current situation as a growth crisis, emphasizing the sharp break between the rapid growth of the 1960s and 1970s and the stagnation of the 1980s. In reality the growth crisis and the debt crisis are two aspects of the same problem, and both growth and debt-servicing capability will have to be restored in Latin America for a full resolution of the problem.

In this study, the first in the Brookings Studies in International Economics series, Thomas O. Enders and Richard P. Mattione address these problems of debt and growth. The authors examine the structure of the Latin American economies and the external and internal shocks that those countries experienced from 1979 to 1982. They then analyze the impact on growth and foreign debt of the various policy options available for confronting the current crisis. They emphasize the likely difficulties in restoring both growth and debt-servicing capabilities during the 1980s and the particular importance of expanded trade between Latin America and the industrialized world in any proposed resolution of Latin America's economic difficulties.

Thomas O. Enders is currently U.S. ambassador to Spain. Richard P. Mattione is a research associate in the Brookings Foreign Policy Studies program. The authors are grateful to Edward M. Bernstein, Jorge Del Canto, Richard J. Herring, and Paul McGonagle for detailed comments on earlier drafts, and to Gerald A. Rosen and Robert L. Glass for their assistance at various stages of the project. They are also grateful to Virginia M. Black, who typed many drafts; to James R. Schneider, who edited the manuscript; and to Bruce Dickson and Alan G. Hoden, who verified its factual content.

The computer projections of chapter three were made possible by the assistance of the Department of State; the study was funded by grants from the National Science Foundation, the Ford Foundation, and the German Marshall Fund.

The views expressed are those of the authors, and should not be ascribed to the U.S. Department of State, to the other individuals and organizations whose assistance is acknowledged above, or to the trustees, officers, or staff members of the Brookings Institution.

BRUCE K. MACLAURY
*President*

*March 1984*
*Washington, D.C.*

THE CRISIS that struck Latin America in 1981–82 has inflicted heavy losses on borrowers, lenders, and industrial countries alike. It has deprived Latin America of growth and has forced lenders to reschedule repayments of principal and in most cases to put up new money. The crisis has also caused a sharp drop in exports from the United States and other industrial countries to Latin America. Cooperation between lenders and borrowers, however, has made it possible thus far to avoid disaster. In fact, many of those attending the September 1983 meetings of the International Monetary Fund and the World Bank felt confident enough to announce that the system was holding. That announcement was perhaps premature. Although the worst has so far been avoided, the situation will not return to normal for a long time. The various participants have not yet even reconciled their contrasting views of the nature of the crisis.

Bankers and government officials in the industrial world essentially consider it a debt crisis. The jeopardy is obvious. Bank loans of $217.9 billion are outstanding to Latin America, representing almost three-fifths of all bank loans outstanding to developing countries at the end of June 1983. Banks and borrowers were negotiating $100.5 billion of reschedulings and new credits during 1983, and major banks from the industrial nations have made loans to the region that far exceed their capital base.[1] The crisis is reflected in the concerns expressed so often in recent months: whether debtors will adopt stabilization measures that can justify new lending from banks and the International Monetary Fund (IMF); whether they will make interest payments or repudiate the debts; whether borrowers will bargain individually or form a cartel. What will be the consequences for the banking system of the industrial world if one or several major debtors should default? Or more optimistically, how long will it be before forced, collective, prorationed new lending to Latin America can be dispensed with

1. As of December 1982 the nine largest U.S. banks had loans outstanding to Latin America equal to 172.2 percent of their capital. Data on Western bank lending are from Bank for International Settlements, *Maturity Distribution of International Bank Lending* (Basle: BIS, December 1983); data on reschedulings are from "The Banks' Rescheduling Schedule," *Institutional Investor–International Edition* (September 1983), pp. 180D–82D. For U.S. data see Federal Financial Institutions Examination Council data reprinted in Federal Reserve Bank of Chicago, *International Letter*, no. 503 (July 1, 1983), p. 3.

and normal transactions between individual banks and borrowers can be reestablished?

Answers to those questions seem to have become less apprehensive over the past year. Mexico took decisive action to improve its current account position, and most countries have accorded a high priority to interest payments. IMF negotiations with Brazil, Argentina, and others have produced new commitments when the original ones were not applied or were judged insufficient. Banks and others have produced studies hopeful that a benign international conjuncture (substantial recovery in the industrial world and no new oil shock) will lower debt-exports ratios and gradually absorb the problem.

Yet Latin Americans are less sanguine. Governments there see a growth crisis. For a generation, in one of the great upward thrusts in history, Latin America grew by almost 6 percent a year in real terms; by 1981 the economy was three times the size it had been in 1960. To take advantage of the jobs that expansion created, armies of people moved from the countryside to the city. When economic growth stopped, unemployment, always a problem with a labor force still growing at the high fertility rates of the 1960s, became severe.[2] Hunger threatens to reach large segments of the population. Given the protests in São Paulo, Rio de Janeiro, Santiago, and Lima, Latin American leaders wonder whether the political system will hold.

Latin Americans are not impressed by the prospects of world recovery. They note that recovery in Europe is lagging and that high interest rates may preclude any recovery from leading to the major rise in commodity prices that Latin America needs (basic commodities account for four-fifths of Latin American exports). They also express skepticism about studies projecting substantial declines in debt-exports ratios because those studies neglect what happens within Latin American economies. Amidst these conflicting economic signals, Latin American governments face a host of difficult policy decisions: whether to cut or abandon interest payments, how to obtain more new funds, and above all how to resume growth.

There are, in other words, two dimensions to the problem: debt-servicing capability and growth. To overcome the crisis, both will have to improve. The fundamental issue is whether recovery of the world economy will itself largely restore sustained growth and reconstitute market-type relationships

2. The Inter-American Development Bank reported that the unemployed and underemployed accounted for over 30 percent of the Latin American labor force at the end of 1982 and that the number was still rising in early 1983. For statistics on growth and employment, see Inter-American Development Bank, *Economic and Social Progress in Latin America, 1983 Report* (Washington, D.C.: IDB, 1983), pp. 115, 125, 345.

2

between lenders and borrowers or whether alternative policies by banks, Latin American nations, and Western governments are necessary.

This study asks three specific questions in the course of addressing that issue. First, is it true that external shocks were largely responsible for the crisis? The answer is no. In the late 1970s and early 1980s Latin American countries borrowed far more than was needed to cover the effects of external shocks on the balance of payments, used the extra funds substantially (although indirectly) to increase the real (inflation-adjusted) value of their currencies, and with the exception of Brazil generally did not attempt to adjust to deteriorating external conditions. Overly expansive and concessive internal policies leading to massive capital flight from Mexico, Venezuela, and Argentina account for the larger part of the crisis. Latin American countries probably could have borrowed much less if their currencies had not appreciated during the 1970s and if public sector deficits had not run out of control. Enough new money might then have been available within established bank exposure limits to ride out the 1981–83 slump.

Second, how long will it take for world recovery, accompanied by IMF-approved stabilization plans and continued lending, to restore growth and improve debt-servicing capability? Even with good luck it will probably take most of the decade. A base-case forecast made on these assumptions puts real GDP in the seven major Latin American countries only 6 percent higher in 1987 than in 1982, a 7 percent drop in per capita income. The debt-exports ratio would fall from 291 percent to 252 percent, which would be helpful but would not be enough in most cases to permit the restoration of normal market relations between creditors and debtors. It is therefore unlikely that the crisis will be largely resolved by 1986, as one recent study suggests.[3] Meanwhile political protest in Latin America, a new oil shock, faltering recovery in the industrial world, or the simple exasperation of endless negotiation and renegotiation of debt terms could at some point in some countries lead to moratoria on interest payments or outright repudiation. The threat of a breakdown in the negotiations seemed very real in Argentina in the spring of 1984.

Third, are there alternative strategies that will yield substantially improved performance? Apparently only one viable alternative exists: an export-led strategy involving small real currency devaluations in Latin America and the maintenance of the status quo (if not a liberalization) in trade practices by the United States and other industrial countries.

An investment-led recovery—that is, further measures to shift resources

3. See William R. Cline, *International Debt and the Stability of the World Economy* (Washington, D.C.: Institute for International Economics, 1983), pp. 121–25.

3

from consumption to investment—will not help much in the short or medium term. Such a scheme fails in most countries because the real problem is the limited availability of foreign exchange for financing needed imports rather than the absence of spare domestic production capacity.

At the other end of the spectrum, debt repudiation appears unlikely to be advantageous, given the probable disruption of trade and payments that would result as creditors attempt to attach goods and funds. Even if one assumes that the costs do not exceed 5 percent of trade, only a few countries would gain. If one assumes losses at the 10 percent level, only one country gains. This does not mean that repudiation will not happen, but only that if it does occur, it would not be likely to solve the growth problem.

Nor is there much relief in major debt restructurings. One common proposal of this type is to stretch principal payments over a generation and to reduce interest payments by one-half. All but two countries would grow less under this proposal than with a mix of reschedulings and stabilization programs similar to those already implemented. Latin America cannot resume growth without new credits. But renewed bank lending would be improbable in the face of significant losses on current loans.

The one alternative that brings substantially higher growth without a deterioration in debt-servicing capability is an export-led recovery based on further small real devaluations. This strategy should appeal to industrial countries because Latin American nations would then be able to use the increased export revenues to increase their own imports from developed countries. For the strategy to succeed, however, would require Latin American governments to do what they have shied away from: face up to the elite and middle classes and enterprises that have all in different ways become dependent on foreign goods, foreign travel, or foreign education and that tend to judge a government's performance by its ability to maintain a high exchange rate. It would also require the industrial countries to avoid imposing new restrictions on Latin American exports, if not to liberalize current restrictions. With this strategy, major growth could resume in this decade.

Providing more official capital, though desirable, is not a general solution. A 4 percent real devaluation over five years might accomplish as much as $25.8 billion in incremental lending. This figure, $25.8 billion beyond current commitments through multilateral and national institutions, far exceeds what industrial countries are now willing and able to raise. That does not mean that funds already promised to the IMF, the World Bank, the Inter-American Development Bank (IDB), and the U.S. Export-Import Bank are not essential. By providing the glue that holds the situation together, official loans have in large measure made it possible to proceed

4

this far toward a solution. And the United States must continue to play a major role in such financings.[4] Lending of this type, however, is a necessary but not a sufficient condition for resolution of the crisis.

It is perhaps not surprising that no strategy appears to improve both growth performance and debt-servicing capability more than the present stabilization plans. But it is surprising that there appears to be only one option to improve growth at the expense of debt-servicing performance. And the best strategy, an export-led recovery, faces profound domestic and foreign obstacles.

In light of this analysis it is clear that the political dangers must be taken seriously. The great shantytowns that look so squalid have also been sites of hope for the many who came out of the countryside to seek personal freedom and economic opportunity. One sees that process at work as a new settlement gradually solidifies from tents to one-story brick structures, then to two-story brick homes, eventually accompanied by motorcycles. Only a few regiments of that great army that moved from the countryside to camp around Latin American cities will be able to return. For these people the change from 6 percent average annual growth to stagnation or negative growth, with all that means in loss of construction and industrial jobs, has dramatic implications. Many are now being pushed into destitution. In some places hunger has become a factor, in others rioting has begun. No one can know how the situation will develop.

The political stresses that are appearing will put at risk the broad but shallow trend toward democracy that has marked the hemisphere in the last five years. First Peru and Ecuador and then Argentina moved away from military regimes to elected governments, more often because of the economic and other failures of the military than for the perceived virtues of representative government. In Brazil a more confident and successful military government has gradually moved toward democracy.

It is unlikely that political tension will recreate the solid, bureaucratic-

4. Those financings include $2.2 billion of mostly overnight drawings by Mexico under regular Federal Reserve System reciprocal currency arrangements; $1.88 billion of Mexican drawings under special swap arrangements; $1.88 billion of Brazilian drawings under special swap arrangements; $1 billion in the form of advance oil payments and $1 billion in agricultural credits to Mexico, later expanded to $1.2 billion of agricultural credits; and promises of new loan guarantees through the Export-Import Bank amounting to $1.5 billion for Brazil and $500 million for Mexico. For details, see Sam Y. Cross, "Treasury and Federal Reserve Foreign Exchange Operations," *Quarterly Review* (Federal Reserve Bank of New York, Summer 1983), pp. 45–49; Peter Montagnon and Alan Friedman, "Central Banks Act Fast to Aid Mexico," *Financial Times*, August 19, 1982; "Mexico's Grain Binge: Buy Now, Pay Never?" *Business Week* (June 13, 1983), p. 35; and Jonathan Fuerbringer, "$2 Billion More in Latin Loans Backed by U.S.," *New York Times*, August 18, 1983.

military governments that came into power in Latin America a generation ago. In most places the military has lost too much prestige during its years in power for that to happen. Rather, the risk is that weakened civilian or military governments will take repressive measures, not necessarily always successfully. The risk, in other words, may well be disorder rather than dictatorship.

It is impossible to forecast these volatile political situations in any detail. Clearly there will be considerable variation from country to country. Mexico has and will retain a government of great authority and strength. Colombia has quite promising economic and political prospects, and despite the stresses, it appears that democracy will hold in Venezuela. But the pressure is rising, and it would be unwise to ignore its existence in a region with over 300 million people and $300 billion in debt. Although the policy options are narrow, effective use of the available opportunities may make the difference between eventual recovery and unrest throughout the hemisphere.

## Capital Import and the Great Expansion of the 1970s

When growth stopped at the end of 1981, the Latin American economy was more than three times the size it had been in 1960. The motor force had come essentially from within the domestic economy, and the motors were the classical ones of growth: manufacturing provided the bulk of the expansion, and power generation, transportation, and financial services grew fastest. Agriculture and mining, however, lagged.[5] The combined share of exports and imports of goods and nonfactor services increased during the two decades from 20.7 percent of GDP in 1970 to 25.6 percent in 1981 (much of that increase, however, was caused by the higher real prices of traded commodities).[6] The physical volume of imports grew faster than real GDP from 1970 to 1980, while the volume of exports grew more slowly than real GDP.[7]

To sustain the growth, Latin America devoted a high and rising share of

5. Inter-American Development Bank, *Economic and Social Progress in Latin America, 1983 Report* (Washington, D.C.: IDB, 1983), p. 117.

6. Nonfactor services exclude interest payments and repatriation of profits from foreign capital. These calculations use national income accounts data for the seven largest countries. See International Monetary Fund, *International Financial Statistics*, vol. 28 (December 1975), and IMF, *International Financial Statistics, 1983 Yearbook* (Washington, D.C.: IMF, 1983).

7. IDB, *Economic and Social Progress in Latin America, 1982 Report* (Washington, D.C.: IDB, 1982), pp. 26–27.

its resources to investment: in the 1960s the share of GDP devoted to investment averaged 20.3 percent and in the 1970s, 23.7 percent. In the 1960s the bulk of investment was financed domestically; from 1965 to 1970 net capital import accounted for 8.8 percent of total investment. But in the next decade massive capital inflows occurred, equal to 20.1 percent of the investment of the 1970s.[8]

This recourse to foreign borrowing did not result solely from initiatives in the borrowing countries. Rather, it could not have occurred without major shifts on the supply side—changes in bank exposure standards in the late 1960s and early 1970s that made Latin America look underborrowed, the subsequent pressure to invest deposits from oil-producing nations, and the apparently negligible real cost of borrowing during the decade-long inflationary upswing in the industrial world. The fact that Latin America borrowed an average of 25 percent more than it needed to cover the current account deficit during the 1970s and built up international reserves in every year of that decade reflects the lack of supply constraints.

At first external borrowings were matched by an increase in investment: in 1974 and 1975 gross investment and foreign financings reached all-time highs of 25.3 percent and 5.47 percent of GDP, respectively. But investment then declined more rapidly than external financing over the rest of the decade, even after correcting for a rise in net interest payments induced partly by Western inflation (table 1). Thus by the end of the decade Latin America had shifted somewhat to a strategy of sustaining growth by using foreign credits to maintain domestic consumption.

Foreign borrowing also helped to moderate inflation. After running at the relatively modest annual rate of 12 percent for Latin America as a whole in the 1960s, price rises accelerated. Many factors contributed: petroleum price shocks, inflation in the industrial countries, increasingly ambitious government investment projects implemented while government savings remained roughly constant, high rates of domestic money creation, and spreading indexation of wages. For the 1970s, Latin American inflation reached an annual rate of 75 percent, and it averaged 128 percent a year in the last four years of the decade.[9]

Foreign borrowing appealed to government officials as a means of avoiding the usually inflationary process of adjusting current account deficits

8. Ratio of net capital inflow, as recorded in the balance of payments, and investment, which in this case the IDB defined as gross physical investment plus changes in net international reserves. See IDB, *Economic and Social Progress in Latin America, 1982 Report*, p. 35.

9. IDB, *Economic and Social Progress in Latin America, 1982 Report*, p. 35.

7

Table 1. *Selected Economic Statistics for Latin America, 1971–80*

| | Annual increase (percent) | | Ratio to GDP (percent) | | | | Index (1970 = 100) |
|---|---|---|---|---|---|---|---|
| Period | Real GDP | Consumer prices | Gross investment | Foreign financing[a] | Net income payments to foreign capital | Current account deficit | Real exchange rate[b] |
| 1971–73 | 7.50 | 12.77 | 22.9 | 3.25 | 1.85 | 2.16 | 97.50 |
| 1974–75 | 5.47 | 94.97 | 25.3 | 5.45 | 2.02 | 3.74 | 87.39 |
| 1976–79 | 5.39 | 127.81 | 23.9 | 4.93 | 2.52 | 3.77 | 87.15 |
| 1980 | 5.73 | 86.82 | 22.2 | 5.21 | 3.34 | 5.04 | 76.20 |

Source: Inter-American Development Bank, *Economic and Social Progress in Latin America, 1982 Report* (Washington, D.C.: IDB, 1983), pp. 35, 44, 56, 70.

a. Balance on the capital account.

b. Weighted between countries by the sum of exports and imports of goods and services. Index represents local currency units per dollar, deflated by consumer price indexes and the U.S. GNP deflator.

through depreciating their currencies or restricting imports. Indeed, it gave countries an opportunity to offset inflation and the negative effects of the petroleum price shocks by an appreciation of real exchange rates: from 1970 to 1980 the average real exchange rate of Latin American currencies rose 31 percent (table 1). Borrowing also offered a means of reducing the inflationary financing of government investment through fiscal deficits or domestic bank credit. But by allowing real currency values to appreciate, and by creating the expectation they would go on appreciating, governments gave enterprises an incentive to borrow abroad rather than at home. Currency overvaluation sharply reduced the cost in local currency of foreign interest payments, and rising overvaluation lowered the costs of amortization.

Finally, foreign borrowing enabled government enterprises to evade budgetary constraints, and they did so on a massive scale in Mexico, Venezuela, Argentina, and Brazil. In 1982, near the end of a long deterioration, those four countries had state enterprise deficits equal to 8.6 percent, 8.3 percent, 5.4 percent, and 5.0 percent of GDP, respectively.[10]

One result of this process was that the overall current account deficit increased from 2.16 percent of GDP in the early 1970s to 3.77 percent of GDP in the late 1970s, then to 5.04 percent and 6.57 percent of GDP in 1980 and 1981. In the 1970s most of this deterioration was caused by higher net imports of goods and noncapital services; less than one-third was caused by increased net payments of interest and profits on foreign capital. This situation was reversed in 1980 and 1981 when 56 percent and 62 percent of the deterioration (relative to the early 1970s) could be explained by increased net payments to foreign capital.[11] Ultimately these current account deficits translated into a gross foreign debt for Latin America that exceeded $300 billion at the end of 1982.[12]

10. See appendix table B-6 for details.

11. See table 1 for data through 1980; for 1981 data see IDB, *Economic and Social Progress in Latin America, 1983 Report*, pp. 345, 369, 373.

12. Data Resources, Inc., has estimated that gross foreign debt equaled $284.9 billion at the end of 1982 in the eight largest Latin American debtors (Argentina, Brazil, Chile, Colombia, Ecuador, Mexico, Peru, and Venezuela). Those eight also accounted for $204.3 billion, or 95.2 percent, of all bank loans to Latin America, according to data from the Bank for International Settlements. If they also accounted for 95.2 percent of all Latin American debt, then gross foreign debt for Latin America would equal $299.5 billion. Because those eight had the best access to bank credits, however, it is likely that their share of overall debt is less than 95.2 percent. In that case Latin America's gross foreign debt could well exceed $300 billion. See Data Resources, Inc., *Latin American Review, Second Quarter 1983* (Lexington, Mass.: DRI, 1983), p. 6; and Bank for International Settlements, *Maturity Distribution of International Bank Lending* (Basle: BIS, July 1983).

It was not inevitable that Latin American nations would have such large current account deficits and foreign debts. One way to have reduced current account deficits and thereby to have limited overall financing requirements would have been to place greater controls on government deficits. True, a given reduction in current account deficits can be achieved by lowering the net financing requirements of either the public or private sectors, which by definition add to the total financing requirement. Evidence from IMF-supported adjustment programs, however, indicates that external imbalances are statistically associated with fiscal imbalances and that reductions and increases in overall government deficits are associated with reductions and increases in the current account deficit. Furthermore, changes in government investment do not appear to be strongly correlated with changes in either total investment or real growth.[13]

Rising real currency values also worsened the current account positions of Latin American nations. If the values had not appreciated, imports would probably have shown smaller increases. (Import volumes increased 100 percent from 1971 to 1980, while real GDP increased 81 percent.)[14] The impact of stable exchange rates on exports would have been smaller because commodities, generally priced in dollars, accounted for approximately 80 percent of exports throughout the decade. Had the real exchange rate been held constant at the start of the 1970s, it is conceivable that imports might have grown no faster than GDP.[15] Net borrowing in that case would have been very substantially less (although not necessarily zero; Latin America started the decade with a current account deficit). Net interest and dividend payments would have risen substantially less, and the current account deficit at the end of the 1970s would have been in the range of 2 to 3 percent of GDP, not 5 percent. In other words, ample borrowing capacity would have been available to bridge the 1981–82 world recession.

13. These results cover a number of Latin American, Asian, and African countries. See Margaret R. Kelly, "Fiscal Adjustment and Fund-Supported Programs, 1971–1980," *IMF Staff Papers*, vol. 29 (December 1982), pp. 561–602.

14. IDB, *Economic and Social Progress in Latin America, 1982 Report*, p. 27.

15. Suppose that the income elasticity of imports in Latin American nations is 1.0; that is, a 1 percent increase in real incomes translates into a 1 percent increase in real imports. Then the 10.9 percent increase in the share of imports in GDP must be due to relative price effects. The 31.2 percent appreciation in local currencies during the course of the decade would imply a price elasticity of −0.38; that is, a 1 percent decrease in the relative price of imports would lead to a 0.38 percent increase in the volume of imports. This is a relatively modest estimate of the import price elasticity for Latin American nations. Khan's 1974 study, for example, yielded price elasticity estimates between −0.63 and −1.98 for eight Latin American countries, though not all of these estimates were statistically significant. (His estimates of income elasticities, however, are usually less than 1.0 in magnitude.) Mohsin S. Khan, "Import and Export Demand in Developing Countries," *IMF Staff Papers*, vol. 21 (1974), pp. 678–93.

How much growth would have been sacrificed if policy changes had reduced borrowings? Borrowing did provide additional real resources. Setting aside increased net interest and dividends, the current account deficit gradually increased until at the end of the decade it was 1.5 percentage points of GDP larger; total supply increased by an equivalent amount. One would expect those resources devoted to investment and intermediate inputs to have had a multiplier effect, increasing demand for construction and other industrial activities. Some of the additional resources might not have contributed to growth, however. For example, it is conceivable that the sharp increase in the share of consumer goods in total imports of goods for Argentina, Mexico, and Chile during the course of the decade was due mostly to appreciation of domestic currencies and therefore did not improve domestic production capabilities.[16] Furthermore, some of what is reported as government investment supported by foreign borrowing might better be characterized as government consumption.

The only conclusion that can be drawn is that if Latin American nations had not chosen to raise real exchange rates of their currencies, they could have obtained those net additional real resources with substantially less borrowing, and their access to credit markets could have continued much longer.

If early implementation of appropriate domestic policies could have reduced or avoided some of the recent disruptions, why were such policies not tried? In most countries the politics of national pride and personality played a role, with political leaders being judged—and judging themselves—by their ability to maintain a strong currency. In early 1982 the Mexican president, in the most striking case of this sort of commitment, pledged to maintain the value of "mi peso," only to refer to himself as "un presidente devaluado" when he could not. But behind personal politics stood the interests of the vast new urban populations, above all those of the capitals, that grew up in the last generation. In some cases—Caracas is the most striking example—capitals came to depend on foreign sources of food. In most they became dependent on foreign consumer goods other than food. Foreign travel, foreign shopping, and foreign property ownership became common prerogatives for the burgeoning middle class. So devaluation would strike at a range of interests that could readily be mobilized to bring pressure on governments. Leader after leader premised his prestige on avoiding devaluation; ultimately, none succeeded.

Exchange rate politics—not only overvaluation but the stop-go cycles

16. For data, see United Nations Economic Commission for Latin America, *Economic Survey of Latin America 1980* (Santiago de Chile: United Nations, 1982), pp. 59, 218, 373.

that result from trying to overvalue and failing—is also one major reason why Latin America, although deriving almost a quarter of its GDP from manufactures, exported so small a part of them. Another is the lack of a systematic orientation toward exports. Nearly all the countries provided a range of export incentives, but those incentives were and are often undone by overvalued currencies, exchange controls, and quantitative restrictions on imports. Thus it is often unclear whether the overall policy promotes exports.[17] Furthermore, in some countries potential exporters were regularly crowded out of access to credit or imported raw materials by large-scale development projects favored by the government. In most cases, manufacturers do not have to face free import competition and may as a result lag in product development and marketing skills.[18] Several other factors suggest the lack of export orientation. Manufactures accounted for around 20 percent of merchandise exports during the 1970s, but two-fifths went to other Latin American countries. In addition, individual product categories show wide swings in volume from year to year, which led one report to suggest that special currency arrangements and shortage or surplus situations may have influenced the trade.[19]

The Latin American experience contrasts sharply with that of the successful export-oriented developing countries of East Asia, which did not overvalue their currencies in the 1970s. While trade in goods and nonfactor services equaled 25.6 percent of GDP in the seven Latin American nations in 1981, it equaled 77.1 percent of GDP in East Asia.[20] And the commodity

17. The importance of the overall policy posture for export promotion can be seen in the calculations of effective exchange rates reported by Krueger, who summarizes a series of country studies done for the National Bureau of Economic Research. See Anne O. Krueger, *Liberalization Attempts and Consequences* (Cambridge, Mass.: Ballinger for the National Bureau of Economic Research, 1978), pp. 69–85.

18. The only thoroughgoing liberalization attempted in the last generation was in Chile. Peru also took some important steps in that direction during its 1978 IMF stabilization program, but experiments by Argentina were soon reversed. Other countries have often imposed new import restrictions during exchange rate crises.

19. These figures, based on the standard international trade statistics, are from IDB, *Economic and Social Progress in Latin America, 1982 Report*, pp. 33, 106–07. The United Nations Industrial Development Organization (UNIDO) has published alternative statistics counting as manufactures all exports that enter the manufacturing component of GDP. This affects particularly the countries exporting minerals (ores often require concentrating and smelting near the source) and foodstuffs and beverages (for which producer countries do some of the less sophisticated processing). These products are still relatively undifferentiated commodities and remain susceptible to sharp swings in prices. On this broader UNIDO basis, 50 percent of Latin America's exports were manufactures in 1970 and only slightly more in 1980. Detailed data using the UNIDO definition are presented in the IDB, *Economic and Social Progress in Latin America, 1982 Report*, pp. 106–40.

20. East Asia is defined here as Indonesia, Malaysia, the Philippines, Singapore, South

12

dependence of merchandise trade is significantly higher in Latin America (table 2). As a result the most important links between the industrial countries and Latin America were the indirect ones of commodity prices and interest rates. The effects on Latin America of the growth of industrial countries therefore tended to bunch during periods of booming commodity prices rather than to act over the whole upswing.

The high growth rates of the 1960s and 1970s made it easy to ignore questions about the sustainability of the Latin American model of development, which was based on import substitution, commodity exports, large-scale state enterprises, and large-scale capital imports. The next two questions are: what brought this development to a halt, and how difficult will it be to get it going again in the changed environment of the 1980s?

What Went Wrong

For Latin America as a whole, growth stopped in 1981, and in 1982 many countries could no longer make repayments of the principal of their debt. In less than two years, full expansion and liquidity had been replaced by stagnation and illiquidity.

There are three competing but not necessarily exclusive explanations for what went wrong. One is that the causes were primarily external to Latin America: the cumulative impact of the 1978–82 surge in interest rates, the second petroleum shock (for oil importers), the deep slide in nonpetroleum commodity prices that began in 1979, and the 1980–82 world recession finally pushed Latin America beyond its borrowing capacity and forced a brutal adjustment. A second explanation is that the causes were largely internal, that Latin America not only failed to adjust to the shocks of the last five years but made them worse. Instead of adopting the classical tactics of adjustment—encouraging exports and further discouraging imports through exchange rate policies, stimulating private savings and cutting down on government deficits, controlling both the investment and current accounts of state-owned enterprises—Latin American governments allowed overly expansive and concessive policies to undercut credit ratings and dry up sources of new money, leaving no alternative to immediate adjustment. A third explanation is that the crisis occurred when surging credit demands collided with lenders' exposure limits, which, however

Korea, and Thailand. The data for Singapore exclude trade in services. No comparable data are available for Hong Kong. See IMF, *International Financial Statistics*, vol. 36 (July 1983).

Table 2. *Dependence on Primary Commodities in Latin America and East Asia, 1960, 1978, 1980*

| Country | Primary commodities (percentage of all merchandise exports) | | |
|---|---|---|---|
| | 1960 | 1978 | 1980 |
| East Asia (seven-country average) | . . . | 49 | 51 |
| Hong Kong | 20 | 3 | 7 |
| Indonesia | 100 | 98 | 98 |
| Malaysia | 94 | 79 | 81 |
| Philippines | 96 | 66 | 63 |
| Singapore | 74 | 54 | 46 |
| South Korea | 86 | 11 | 10 |
| Thailand | 98 | 75 | 71 |
| Latin America (seven-country average) | . . . | 79 | 76 |
| Argentina | 96 | 74 | 77 |
| Brazil | 97 | 66 | 61 |
| Chile | 96 | 95 | 80[a] |
| Colombia | 98 | 83 | 80 |
| Mexico | 88 | 70 | 61[a] |
| Peru | 99 | 89 | 84 |
| Venezuela | 100 | 98 | 98 |

Source: World Bank, *World Development Report, 1980; 1981; 1982; 1983* (Washington, D.C.: World Bank), tables 8, 9, and 10.
a. 1979 data.

much they had expanded in the 1970s and however little they had been articulated, had always existed.

Judgments as to how much weight to give each of these arguments underlie the debate on what should now be done to overcome the crisis and to prevent its recurrence. Advocates of a substantial increase in IMF quotas tend to emphasize the external causes of the crisis and the desirability of allowing more time and more scope for adjustment. Proponents of a debtors' cartel believe commercial banks caused the crisis, charging that the banks first encouraged Latin America to believe it could borrow almost at will and then abruptly and collectively withheld access to new money. Similarly, both opponents of increased IMF resources and promoters of curbs on U.S. bank lending to developing countries charge the banks with complacency if not malfeasance. And in the ongoing bargaining over how the burden of adjustment is to be divided up, the banks and governments, of course, emphasize each other's management errors.

Judgment as to how difficult it will be to resume growth in Latin America also depends in part on what one thinks went wrong. If external shocks alone account for the crisis, it may now be well on the way to being resolved, with interest rates and petroleum prices down, the U.S. economy recovering, and the potential for higher commodity prices as the recovery spreads. Similarly, if herd behavior by the bankers first encouraged Latin American governments to put off adjustments to the shocks and then abruptly forced them to carry out those adjustments, herd behavior could also cause the bankers to return as confidence recovers.[21]

If overly expansive and concessive domestic policies played a key role, it may be harder to predict how long and how much effort the return to sustained growth in Latin America will require. Stabilization programs are just now being implemented, and there is limited information on which to base predictions of how well they will do. Clearly, to the degree that internal causes have dominated, the road back could be longer and more difficult than many may now expect.

### External Causes

There can be no doubt about the power of the shocks that have struck Latin America in the last five years: rising oil prices, falling prices for other commodities, deteriorating terms of trade, low demand for Latin American exports because of Western recession, and high real interest rates all had a significant impact.[22]

Latin America rode out the first petroleum shock and the subsequent world recession of 1974–75 without losing its dynamism, its self-confidence, or its credit ratings. Growth faltered and then recovered, although not to pre-1973 levels. The current account deficit grew sharply and then began to fall. Export volumes rose sharply after 1975—more than 25 percent over three years. The structure of its foreign public debt, having shifted at first toward loans with shorter maturities, stabilized and then began to move toward longer maturities.[23] Spreads (the difference between what borrowers pay on bank loans and what banks pay for the Eurodollar

21. Of course, such herd behavior should be discouraged in good times and bad. Various regulatory measures are available that would help to keep banks from being too expansionary in their future foreign lending activities. See Richard S. Dale and Richard P. Mattione, *Managing Global Debt* (Brookings Institution, 1983), pp. 34–39.

22. The terms of trade is the ratio of prices received by a country for its exports to prices it pays for imports. Thus deteriorating terms of trade means that export prices for a given country are falling relative to import prices.

23. Inter-American Development Bank, *Economic and Social Progress in Latin America, 1980–81 Report* (Washington, D.C.: IDB, 1981), pp. 7, 43, 46, 98.

Table 3. *External Shocks for Seven Latin American Countries, 1979–1982*

| | Percentage of GDP | | | | | Cumulative (billions of dollars) | Cumulative share of trade[a] (percent) |
|---|---|---|---|---|---|---|---|
| Country | 1979 | 1980 | 1981 | 1982 | Cumulative | | |
| Colombia | -2.79 | -3.48 | -5.58 | -7.13 | -4.94 | -6.8 | -22.7 |
| Brazil | -1.43 | -3.78 | -5.73 | -6.52 | -4.56 | -48.5 | -30.1 |
| Chile | 1.97 | -0.06 | -7.93 | -10.89 | -4.61 | -4.8 | -14.9 |
| Argentina | 0.11 | -2.26 | -3.72 | -8.26 | -3.00 | -13.4 | -21.9 |
| Peru | 2.46 | 3.01 | 0.72 | -2.69 | 0.53 | 0.4 | 1.6 |
| Mexico | 0.24 | 1.76 | 1.63 | 2.47 | 1.60 | 11.7 | 8.8 |
| Venezuela | 5.40 | 9.99 | 9.87 | 5.58 | 7.79 | 19.1 | 16.6 |

Source: Authors' calculations, detailed in appendix A.
Note: A minus sign indicates an unfavorable shock. Cumulative shock adds up the 1979–82 figures in current dollars without adjusting for dollar inflation.
a. Trade consists of exports and imports of goods only.

deposits funding those loans) for all developing-country borrowers increased in 1976 but had decreased sharply by 1979.[24]

In 1978, on the eve of the second oil shock, it seemed that Latin America had adjusted successfully to the post-oil-shock world. For this reason 1976–78 was chosen as the base period in calculating the magnitude of the external shocks of 1979–82. This part of the study focuses on the seven largest countries—Argentina, Brazil, Chile, Colombia, Mexico, Peru, and Venezuela—which together produce 90 percent of the region's GDP and are also the largest borrowers. Four categories of shocks are calculated for each country; in all four categories a positive number denotes a favorable shock.

First, the terms-of-trade shock is calculated. It has two components. The difference between export prices in a given year and base-period export prices corrected for Western (dollar) inflation, multiplied by current export volumes, shows the part of the shock caused by export price shifts. Similarly, the difference between base-period import prices corrected for inflation and actual import prices, multiplied by current import volumes, shows the shock due to import price shifts. These two numbers are combined to yield the total terms-of-trade shock facing a country. Next, a separate calculation is made for oil price shocks because of the importance attached to the oil price increases of 1979–82 in explanations of Latin America's difficulties. This measure, too, corrects revenues or expenditures for the difference between base-period oil prices corrected for inflation and actual oil prices. In all these calculations of terms-of-trade shocks, current volumes (total exports, total imports, and exports or imports of oil) are taken as a given.

The third component measures the effects of Western recession on the demand for Latin America's non-oil exports. Oil exports are excluded from the calculation because a significant part of the shortfall in volume reflected the deliberate decisions of oil producers. The final component of the calculated external shocks reflects high real interest rates. The measure of these shocks represents the difference between real interest rates in the base period and in the current year multiplied by bank debt outstanding at the beginning of the current year.

Tables 3 and 4 present summary data on the external shocks experienced by the seven countries from 1979 to 1982.[25] The nature of the shocks

24. World Bank, *World Development Report, 1980* (Washington, D.C.: World Bank, 1980), p. 27.

25. See appendix A for more information on the method of calculation and on data sources.

facing each country varies considerably. For Argentina, Brazil, Chile, and Colombia the net effect was unfavorable; it was favorable for Mexico, Peru, and Venezuela. All countries were harmed by high real interest rates and low demand for their exports. The terms-of-trade shock, or more specifically high oil prices, thus explains much of the difference in the experiences of the two groups.

By some measures Brazil was the country hardest hit; its $48.5 billion shock was equal to 30.1 percent of merchandise trade. Oil price increases accounted for more than one-third of the total impact, but Brazil suffered in all other categories. Colombia, however, experienced the largest cumulative shock as a share of GDP, while Chile experienced the biggest shift over time. Argentina experienced smaller unfavorable shocks than the other three.

Venezuela was the most favored country, with the annual positive shock peaking at 10 percent of GDP and a 1979–82 average equal to 16.6 percent of merchandise trade. Mexico shows smaller favorable shocks in relation to GDP, while in Peru unfavorable shocks in 1982 undid most of the favorable ones of earlier years.

In most cases the external shocks had a heavy impact on trade. They also represented a significant share of GDP, despite the fact that trade is less important to these economies than, for example, to Asian nations. In every case the terms-of-trade shock had the dominant effect, reflecting both Latin America's high dependence on commodity exports and the transcendent importance of oil as an import or export in all but two of the cases studied. The interest rate shock accounts for less than one-third of the total impact on each of the four countries adversely affected during this period. For the other three its magnitude is less than half of the favorable terms-of-trade shock (table 4).

### Internal Causes

How is it possible to judge whether a country acted to adjust to successive shocks and whether the actions taken improved its situation or made it worse? A first approximation can be achieved by comparing the estimated magnitude of the external shock with the deterioration or (in the case of positive shocks) improvement in the current account. If a country faced a worsening situation but the current account deteriorated by an amount less than that of the estimated shocks, the country is defined as having actively adjusted; otherwise it compounded its external shocks. If the current account of any country receiving favorable shocks improved by an amount up

18

**Table 4.** *Sources and Magnitude of Shocks for Seven Latin American Countries, 1979–82*

Billions of dollars

| Country | Total | Changes in terms of trade | | High real interest rates | Low export demand |
| --- | --- | --- | --- | --- | --- |
| | | All trade | Oil trade | | |
| Colombia | −6.8 | −4.3 | −0.9 | −0.9 | −1.6 |
| Brazil | −48.5 | −31.7 | −17.9 | −8.9 | −7.9 |
| Chile | −4.8 | −1.9 | −1.4 | −1.5 | −1.5 |
| Argentina | −13.4 | −6.2 | −0.6 | −3.7 | −3.6 |
| Peru | 0.4 | 2.3 | 1.2 | −0.8 | −1.1 |
| Mexico | 11.7 | 22.5 | 21.0 | −8.4 | −2.4 |
| Venezuela | 19.1 | 24.0 | 29.4 | −4.6 | −0.3 |

Source: Authors' calculations.
Note: A minus sign indicates an unfavorable shock. Totals are unadjusted for dollar inflation.

to that of the the shocks, the country actively adjusted. If a country should so expand as to overrun the mark and turn the current account gain into a net deterioration, however, then internal expansion has swamped external improvement.

Such classifications are necessarily imperfect. First, a country's previous situation matters. At the time of the second oil shock, Brazil was already running a $7 billion current account deficit. Because it had little choice, it began to adjust in 1981; others were less constrained.

Second, appropriate behavior depends in part on whether the shock is viewed as temporary or permanent. Countries are likely to want to finance a temporary negative shock or bank a temporary windfall. Such behavior is inappropriate, however, in the face of permanent changes. A permanent deterioration in the external situation requires a permanent downward adjustment of consumption that should not be unduly delayed. On the other hand, a permanent improvement in the external situation may encourage a country to borrow abroad, especially if additional investment funds are needed to realize future prospects more efficiently.[26] Mexico, for instance, probably considered the oil price rises a permanent improvement in its economic outlook and therefore turned to foreign borrowings to finance more ambitious plans for oil production and economic development.

Third, not only does calculation of the shocks necessarily involve assumptions and approximations, but it is impossible to isolate fully external and internal factors in calculating external shocks. Autonomous variations in domestic investment opportunities, for example, and some of the results

26. For further details see Jeffrey D. Sachs, "The Current Account and Macroeconomic Adjustment in the 1970s," *Brookings Papers on Economic Activity*, 1:1981, pp. 215–25.

Table 5. *Overall Adjustment/Disadjustment to External Shocks for Seven Latin American Countries, 1979–82*
Billions of dollars

| Country | Results of shock | 1979 | 1980 | 1981 | 1982 | Cumulative[a] |
|---|---|---|---|---|---|---|
| Colombia | Shock | -0.8 | -1.2 | -2.1 | -2.8 | -6.8 |
| | Current account change[b] | * | -1.1 | -2.5 | -3.0 | -6.6 |
| | Capital export[c] | -0.1 | 0.3 | 0.5 | * | 0.7 |
| Brazil | Shock | -3.3 | -9.4 | -16.5 | -19.3 | -48.5 |
| | Current account change[b] | -4.1 | -6.0 | -4.7 | -8.8 | -23.6 |
| | Capital export[c] | 1.3 | 1.6 | -0.3 | -0.7 | 2.0 |
| Chile | Shock | 0.4 | * | -2.6 | -2.6 | -4.8 |
| | Current account change[b] | -0.7 | -1.5 | -4.3 | -1.9 | -8.5 |
| | Capital export[c] | 0.4 | 0.5 | 0.9 | -0.8 | 1.0 |
| Argentina | Shock | * | -3.5 | -4.6 | -5.4 | -13.4 |
| | Current account change[b] | -2.1 | -6.5 | -5.9 | -4.4 | -18.9 |
| | Capital export[c] | 1.7 | -2.3 | -8.7 | -5.0 | -14.3 |
| Peru | Shock | 0.3 | 0.5 | * | -0.5 | 0.4 |
| | Current account change[b] | 1.5 | 0.9 | -0.6 | -0.5 | 1.3 |
| | Capital export[c] | * | 0.2 | 0.5 | 0.6 | 1.3 |
| Mexico | Shock | 0.3 | 3.3 | 3.9 | 4.2 | 11.7 |
| | Current account change[b] | -2.8 | -4.8 | -10.1 | -1.0 | -18.7 |
| | Capital export[c] | -0.8 | -1.1 | -4.9 | -8.3 | -15.2 |
| Venezuela | Shock | 2.6 | 5.9 | 6.7 | 3.9 | 19.1 |
| | Current account change[b] | 3.6 | 8.3 | 7.9 | -0.2 | 19.5 |
| | Capital export[c] | 2.4 | -3.1 | -4.9 | -7.4 | -13.0 |

Source: Authors' calculations; see appendix A for details.
*Between -$0.05 billion and $0.05 billion.
a. Figures may not add because of rounding.
b. Adjusted for inflation.
c. A minus sign denotes capital flight, that is, an unfavorable movement in the relevant items of the capital account.

of internal policy steps—particularly anything affecting the volume of imports—could influence the estimate of the impact of terms-of-trade changes.

Finally, capital flight is particularly important in evaluating a country's response to external shocks. Mexico, Argentina, and Venezuela seriously aggravated their financing problem by inducing and in some cases facilitating capital flight (table 5). Therefore estimates of short-term, private capital export are included along with the calculations of current account deterioration to give a more accurate picture of the total financing gap. Figure 1 therefore provides two measures of the adjustment efforts of the major Latin American countries. The first ratio compares the inflation-adjusted change in the current account to the magnitude of the external shock. The second compares adjustment in the total financing requirement (inflation-adjusted current account change minus capital flight) to the magnitude of the external shock.

There is an extraordinary diversity of behavior. Contrary to the impression that became widespread when the debt crisis broke in 1982, terms-of-trade changes and high real interest rates were not common factors that brought these countries to grief all at once. It is of course true that the reaction to the shocks of the late 1970s and early 1980s depends partly on the 1976–78 starting point assumed. Peru, for instance, probably reduced its total financing requirement by more than the positive shock it received to offset the large current account deficits of the mid-1970s. Similarly, Colombia's low debt and history of good current account performance enabled it to make little adjustment. After the second oil shock, Venezuela did not expand as much as it might have because of constraints imposed by earlier current account deficits.

No country completely offset the impact of negative shocks. Brazil made the greatest effort at adjustment, while Colombia was about neutral. Internal policy decisions in Chile and Argentina substantially compounded the effects of a worsening external environment.

The countries receiving a favorable shock performed in very different ways. Venezuela's current account performance seems acceptable, but much of that adjustment was undone by capital flight resulting from failures of business confidence and from an artificially high exchange rate. Peru's very strong actions can be explained by the severe imbalances incurred from 1976 to 1978, but not by conditions from 1979 to 1982. Mexico, no doubt persuaded that the price of petroleum would go on advancing, saw its balance of payments deteriorate sharply despite the favorable shocks.

21

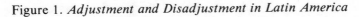

Figure 1. *Adjustment and Disadjustment in Latin America*

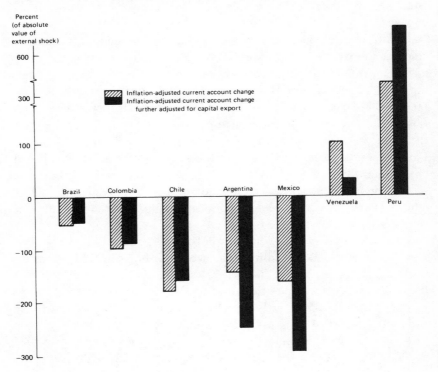

For these countries as a whole, internal causes of the crisis were more significant than were external causes. The net total shock was $42.3 billion. But the total incremental financing requirement came to $93.2 billion, $55.7 billion in increased current account deficits after correcting for inflation and $37.5 billion in estimated capital export.

Whether a country applied protectionist or liberal trade policies appears not to have influenced the outcome. Two of the most protected economies, Mexico and Brazil, behaved quite differently, the former expanding explosively and the latter moving toward adjustment. Two of the most liberal, Chile and (at least part of the time) Argentina, turned in poor adjustment records. In both these latter cases, however, trade liberalization measures were accompanied by unrealistic exchange rates.

Finally, the notion that adjustment to unfavorable shocks leads unavoidably to reduced growth, while increased spending in all cases leads to further growth, finds little support in the experiences of these seven nations. As table 6 shows, only Brazil can easily fit this simple story. Mexico and

Table 6. *Adjustment and Growth in Seven Latin American Countries, 1975–82*

| Country | Policy stance 1979–82[a] | Cumulative growth 1975–78 (percent) | 1979–82 (percent) |
|---|---|---|---|
| Negative shock received | | | |
| Colombia | Neutral | 24.1 | 13.8 |
| Brazil | Adjuster | 28.0 | 11.5 |
| Chile | Disadjuster | 7.2 | 3.4 |
| Argentina | Disadjuster | 1.5 | -3.9 |
| Positive shock received | | | |
| Peru | Adjuster | 3.3 | 6.4 |
| Mexico | Disadjuster | 23.3 | 27.2 |
| Venezuela | Neutral | 26.3 | 1.1 |

Sources: Data for 1979–82 are from Data Resources, Inc., *Latin America Review, Second Quarter 1983* (Lexington, Mass.: DRI, 1983). Data for 1975–78 are from International Monetary Fund, *International Financial Statistics, 1983 Yearbook* (Washington, D.C.: IMF, 1983).

a. As indicated by the ratio of current account deterioration to the value of the external shock.

Colombia fit less well, and in the other cases the supposed relationship was overwhelmed by more basic factors. Unable to sustain the confidence of private investors and yet not successful in investing in public enterprise at a profit, Venezuela failed absolutely to convert this second petroleum shock into growth. Chile was overly reliant on foreign credits and generated only minimal private domestic savings; it saw much of the growth achieved undone when overseas lenders stopped providing new credits. Unable to achieve a durable consensus on policy, Argentina could not prevent both a drastic fall in savings and a hemorrhage of capital flight.

### Country Patterns

To appreciate the interplay of the various internal and external causes, it is useful to examine in more depth the patterns of response, or lack of response, of the individual countries.[27]

Brazil kept its incremental financing requirements below the level of the external shock by reacting relatively quickly to the second oil shock. In 1979 and 1980 it initiated a substantial adjustment program, including a so-called maxidevaluation of the cruzeiro, monetary and fiscal restraint, and a liberalization of the foreign trade system (the latter designed to

27. The analysis in this section is based on many sources: the tables presented here and in appendix B, other sources described in appendix A, and policy summaries prepared by the Inter-American Development Bank and available in the "Country Summaries" section of the 1980–81, 1982, and 1983 reports, *Economic and Social Progress in Latin America*.

capture the efficiency gains of the devaluation). By 1981 the combined impact of the large-scale negative shocks and the adjustment effort had brought growth to a halt. Yet stagnation did not bring the expected improvement in external accounts. Instead, the real value of the cruzeiro was allowed to rise again to its 1978 level until another maxidevaluation was made in February 1983. Inflation soared to annual rates of around 100 percent in 1981 and 1982. Repeated efforts to bring the deficits of public enterprises under control yielded little result, and their overall deficit rose progressively to 5 percent of GDP in 1982. Gross domestic savings as a share of GDP drifted downward throughout the period, perhaps as a result of high inflation, but so did gross domestic investment. As a result, the current account deficit as a percentage of GDP held about constant but was not significantly reduced. In other words the country had adjusted enough to contain the problem but not enough to resolve it.

In early 1983 Brazil and the IMF agreed on a loan of SDR 4.955 billion ($5.3 billion).[28] Brazil also obtained new loan commitments of $4.4 billion from commercial banks at about the same time. In return the government committed the country over the 1983–85 period to substantial trade surpluses, a sharp reduction in current account deficits and public sector borrowings, and a slowing of inflation.[29] Brazil's inability to meet the terms of the adjustment program led to a suspension of loan disbursements by banks and the IMF in the spring of 1983. A new and milder program, accompanied by reschedulings of Western government credits and a new $6.5 billion loan from commercial banks, was agreed on in the fall of 1983.[30] That new loan was signed in January 1984, though apparently not all of Brazil's bank creditors participated in making the loan.[31]

In this analysis Colombia's adjustment performance is neutral; it borrowed about as much additional money as the cumulative shock. Colombia is heavily dependent on coffee exports and took a variety of countercyclical actions following the break in coffee prices in 1977. The impact was cushioned by lowering both the minimum exchange surrender requirement for

28. The Special Drawing Right, or SDR, is a composite currency used to denominate IMF transactions with its members. SDR amounts in this section were converted at SDR 1 = $1.07. The value of the SDR fluctuated between $1.04 and $1.09 during 1983.

29. See "Fund Approves Package of Assistance for Brazil Totaling SDR 5 Billion," *IMF Survey* (March 7, 1983), pp. 65, 76; and "Brazil Seeks to Strengthen External Position and Re-Evaluate Strategy for Resumed Growth," *IMF Survey* (March 21, 1983), pp. 92–94.

30. See "The High Cost of Keeping Brazil Afloat," *Business Week* (June 6, 1983), p. 27; and Peter Montagnon and Andrew Whitley, "West Agrees to Delay on Brazilian Debt," *Financial Times*, November 24, 1983.

31. See Kenneth N. Gilpin, "Brazil Gets $6.5 Billion in New Loans," *New York Times*, January 28, 1984.

coffee exports and the ad valorem coffee tax. Subsequently the real value of the peso was allowed to increase. In 1979 a broad, government-led investment program in infrastructure was inaugurated; private investment in mining, energy, and manufacturing held steady, while private savings declined. The government also restored positive real returns in the financial system as part of an effort to persuade exporters to repatriate foreign exchange that earlier anti-inflation efforts had driven out. Moreover, the rate of growth in the money supply was reduced and earlier experiments in trade liberalization renewed. Even with these countervailing actions, however, the growth of the economy slowed sharply from a peak of 9 percent in 1978 to 1 percent in 1982, while the current account deficit increased about in proportion to the costs of the estimated shocks, a cumulative equivalent of 4.9 percentage points of GDP.

Colombia signed a $210 million loan with commercial banks in November 1983, and syndication of a $370 million loan for the national electricity utility was still in progress at the end of 1983.[32] So far this continuing access to foreign credit markets combined with drawdowns of foreign currency reserves has allowed Colombia to follow somewhat easier monetary and fiscal policies than other Latin American nations and to avoid an IMF program.

Chile was a substantial disadjuster, running a current account deficit some 77 percent larger than the estimated value of the shocks. Chile's economy expanded at very high levels until mid-1981, fueled by significant increases in private investment activity in spite of flagging exports. Because gross domestic private savings were very low throughout the period, peaking at only 2.9 percent of GDP in 1979, it was necessary to finance the expansion by government surpluses and by a very heavy reliance on foreign credits. Before the start of the crisis in mid-1981, most policies emphasized expansion. Trade was liberalized, the financial system was decontrolled, and access to foreign lending was facilitated. The real money and quasi-money supply increased. Real interest rates tended to decline but remained substantially positive. Capital inflows exceeded the current account deficit by a large margin. At the same time the real value of the peso was allowed to appreciate some 30 percent. When it came, the crisis had a nineteenth-century quality about it: it was a classic crisis of confidence. Concerned by rising consumption and the deteriorating balance of payments, foreign lenders began cutting back disbursements and new commitments. Real

32. See Peter Montagnon, "Colombia Deal Expected," *Financial Times*, October 27, 1983; and Robert Graham, "New Colombian Law Enables Betancur to Seek Further Loans," *Financial Times*, December 20, 1983.

interest rates soared. As activity slowed, the public sector surplus, the main source of domestic savings, also declined. Gross national savings fell by 6.1 percentage points of GDP from 1980 to 1981, and a massive drop in GDP (14.1 percent in 1982) left a still enormous current account deficit. Thus overdependence on foreign capital and failure to start adjusting until foreign leaders forced the issue resulted in the collapse.

The IMF agreed to lend Chile SDR 795 million ($851 million) in January 1983. Of this amount, SDR 500 million was in the form of a two-year standby arrangement. The required adjustment program emphasized domestic credit ceilings to slow inflation, target levels for foreign currency reserves, and limits on the fiscal deficit. But Chile quickly ran into problems, which led to a renegotiation of the IMF program. That new program has basically continued on track. Chile has also reached agreement with commercial banks on the rescheduling of old loans and the provision of new ones. Finally, the banks' advisory committee agreed to make $780 million of new credits with longer maturities and lower interest charges available to Chile during 1984.[33]

Argentina shows a different sort of disadjustment. Its total foreign financial requirement exceeded the estimated cost of the external shocks by 148 percent, primarily because of capital flight. Repeated and complex changes of policy failed to inspire confidence. From 1979 to 1981 both gross private savings and gross domestic investment remained roughly constant at high levels. But the public sector balance deteriorated by 7.3 percentage points of GDP as accelerating inflation caused a lag in receipts, an increase in current outlays, and rising interest payments. The combined effects of the higher real value of the peso, rising real interest rates, and trade liberalization aggravated the situation until 1980. Undoubtedly the Falklands-Malvinas war also played a crucial role. The external shocks were smaller in relation to the size of the economy (about two-thirds as large as those in Brazil, Colombia, and Chile), but the failure to control the finances of the public sector led to severe internal shocks.

Argentina and the IMF agreed on a loan of SDR 2.02 billion ($2.16 billion) in January 1983. Of this amount, SDR 1.5 billion was in the form of a fifteen-month standby arrangement. That standby loan required an adjustment program aimed especially at reducing public sector deficits and

33. See "Chile: Stand-By Arrangement and Compensatory Financing Facility," *IMF Survey* (January 24, 1983), p. 19; Peter Montagnon, "Chile Bid to Hammer Out Rescheduling Agreement," *Financial Times*, March 29, 1983; Robert Graham, "Chile May Readjust Loan Target," *Financial Times*, November 22, 1983; "Refinancing Pact Signed by Chile, Lenders," *Washington Post*, January 26, 1984; and "Chile to Get $780 Million in New Loans from Banks," *Wall Street Journal*, February 23, 1984.

inflation. Commercial banks had arranged a short-term loan of $1.1 billion at about the same time, and later in 1983 agreed to a $1.5 billion medium-term commercial bank loan. Payments arrears and other problems have delayed some of the planned disbursements of funds. Argentina opened negotiations with the IMF for a new $1.5 billion loan in January 1984.[34]

Of the seven countries, Venezuela, heavily dependent on oil exports, received the biggest (and most favorable) shocks relative to its economy, but strikingly, it failed to convert them into growth. When the second oil shock hit in 1979, the government used the additional revenue to rectify the financial imbalances left by the first shock and the subsequent effort to convert new oil wealth into other forms of wealth. Emphasis shifted to expansion in 1980, then to restraint in 1981. Renewed efforts to stimulate the economy in 1982 resulted in very large fiscal and payments deficits. These stop-go policies appear only to have aggravated the weakening of gross private investment, which fell by more than 10 percentage points of GDP from 1979 to 1982, reflecting an extreme lack of confidence in Venezuela's current and prospective policies. Against this background the sustained rise in the real foreign exchange value of the bolivar—otherwise an appropriate reaction to a positive shock—did help to keep inflation down, but it also induced increased imports and capital outflows without contributing to growth.

The combination of expansive public policies and a recessionary private economy ultimately proved untenable. Election year politics made it difficult for the government to approach the IMF for assistance, but Venezuela devalued its currency sharply in early 1983 and set up a three-tier exchange rate system. It broke off talks with the IMF in August 1983, however, over IMF insistence on a further devaluation and a simplification of the exchange rate controls. Although talks on rescheduling with commercial banks remain on hold, the early actions of the new administration suggest that renegotiation of the foreign debt has top priority.[35] The country's substantial foreign exchange reserves have allowed it to delay rescheduing for so long.

34. For details, see "Stand-By Arrangement, Compensatory Financing Approved for Argentina," *IMF Survey* (February 7, 1983), pp. 38–39; Stewart Fleming, "Argentina's Failure to Meet Loan Criteria Worries Banks," *Financial Times*, October 13, 1983; James L. Rowe, Jr., "Report on Argentina Startles Its Lenders," *Washington Post*, December 18, 1983; and Clyde H. Farnsworth, "Argentina Outlines Debt Plan," *New York Times*, January 13, 1984.

35. See Peter Montagnon, "Caracas, IMF Abandon Hope of Early Pact," *Financial Times*, August 30, 1983, and "Venezuela Banking Creditors Divided on Debt Package," *Financial Times*, September 1, 1983; and James Le Moyne, "New Venezuela Leader Sees Debt as No. 1 Issue," *New York Times*, December 12, 1983.

The experience of Mexico, also dependent on oil revenues, contrasts with that of Venezuela. Mexico went all out for growth, and by that criterion it was highly successful; at the end of 1982 the economy was 25 percent larger than it had been four years earlier. Despite the decline in output during 1983, the net gains are impressive. Gross private investment as a share of GDP held steady through 1981, while public investment grew sharply. Fiscal policy became even more expansive (from 1978 to 1982 the share of government savings in GDP swung from positive to negative by 9.6 percentage points of GDP). Monetary policy accommodated the deficits, and inflation accelerated to 100 percent a year. The real foreign exchange value of the peso appreciated sharply, and import restrictions were liberalized until mid-1982. Perhaps most remarkable of all, the share of private sector savings in GDP increased by more than 8 percentage points, advancing even in the crisis year of 1982, when savings rates were falling in most other Latin American nations. This strength may reflect the wide inequalities in the distribution of income and a dramatic increase in income of the wealthiest Mexicans. Without growing private savings the boom would have come to an end much sooner. The first significant sign of trouble was probably the tortuous political maneuvering involved in the attempt to lower the price of Mexico's oil in response to deteriorating oil market conditions during 1981. The boom was terminated in mid-1982 by a combination of vast fiscal and payments deficits, large-scale capital flight, and the drying up of foreign credit.

Mexico had to turn to the U.S. government and to the Bank for International Settlements for emergency credits in August 1982. In December 1982 it concluded a loan of SDR 3.61 billion ($3.86 billion) with the IMF. This included a three-year, extended-financing facility loan of SDR 3.41 billion, in return for which Mexico agreed to a sharp cutback in the overall public sector deficit, reductions in the current account deficit, and progressively lower levels of inflation. Commercial banks arranged $5 billion in new loans in February 1983, and the country had rescheduled $23 billion of debts by December 1983. Mexico's progress in reschedulings and in the IMF program has been relatively smooth; in recognition of this progress, in early 1984 bankers were trying to arrange a new $3.8 billion loan on much easier terms.[36]

36. For details, see Peter Montagnon and Alan Friedman, "Central Banks Act Fast to Aid Mexico," *Financial Times*, August 19, 1982; Sam Y. Cross, "Treasury and Federal Reserve Foreign Exchange Operations," *Quarterly Review* (Federal Reserve Bank of New York, Summer 1983), pp. 45–49; "Mexico to Use Resources from Fund to Support Major Adjustment Effort," *IMF Survey* (January 10, 1983), pp. 1–3; James L. Rowe, Jr., and Caroline Atkinson, "Mexico's Debt Crisis Abates Markedly," *Washington Post*, June 28,

Peru improved its financial position from 1979 to 1982 and did so by more than the amount of the positive shock itself. That calculation says as much about events in the 1976–78 base period—which concluded with the 1978 IMF program that started the process of adjustment—as about the policies of the 1979–82 years. From 1979 to 1982 many of Peru's experiences were similar to those of the other countries: sustained increases in private and public investments, declining private savings, increasing fiscal deficits, and high inflation. What is different is exchange rate policy—the real foreign exchange value of the sol declined continuously from 1978 in spite of the positive shocks and Peru's ability to prolong growth through 1982. Finally in 1983, export shortfalls, the devastation of agricultural production by the El Niño natural disaster, and the limited availability of new credit forced a decline in GDP and a reduction of imports. In effect the small positive shocks, equivalent to only 0.5 percent of GDP on average, were swamped by other, more powerful forces.

Peru arranged a loan of SDR 849.9 million ($909.4 million) from the IMF in June 1982; this included SDR 650 million in the form of a three-year extended facility arrangement. In return, it promised to limit the public sector deficit and to encourage domestic savings and investment. The country also arranged $830 million in commercial bank financing (rescheduling and new loans) and a $1 billion Paris Club rescheduling in the summer of 1983. Banks delayed disbursement of the last $200 million of their loan because of Peru's difficulties in meeting the targets of its IMF loan agreement. Disbursements were expected to resume in early 1984, following new negotiations with the Fund. Peru also has been promised better refinancing terms in 1984, with longer maturities and lower interest charges on $1.5 billion of principal payments originally due during 1984 and 1985. This promise may have partly reflected Peru's decision not to ask for new loans in 1984.[37]

1983; Peter Montagnon, "Mexico Stands by Debt Accord," *Financial Times*, December 22, 1983; and "Mexico Waits on $3.8 Billion Loan Decision," *Financial Times*, January 23, 1984.

37. See "Peru: Extended Arrangement and Compensatory Financing Facility," *IMF Survey* (June 21, 1982), p. 187; S. Karene Witcher, "Fed Ruling May Ease Big Loan to Pemex; Some Lenders Jittery on Peru's Economy," *Wall Street Journal*, July 6, 1983; "Peru Gets Approval to Delay Payments on $1 Billion in Debt," *Wall Street Journal*, July 27, 1983; William Chislett, "Debt Turns Peru Recovery into Game of Chance," *Financial Times*, January 5, 1984; and "Peru Wins Better Terms on Financing Package," *Wall Street Journal*, February 10, 1984.

Public sector deficits played a critical role in creating internal shocks in these economies. These deficits were the most dynamic factor in the period, swinging negatively in the seven countries by 7.83 percentage points of GDP over the four-year period (the net unfavorable external shock was equal to 3.31 percent of GDP).[38]

The rate of private savings was less directly subject to policy decision. Private savings decreased in every country except Mexico in this period. One cause of decreased private saving could have been the stagnant or falling economic activity in 1981 and 1982. And high real exchange rates may also have contributed by encouraging consumers and industries to import goods in anticipation of future devaluations. If it survives the austerity of 1983, the high savings rate could be the single most hopeful element in Mexico's outlook. For others the savings rate is a potentially serious weakness.

More amenable to revision is the real exchange rate. Argentina, Chile, Mexico, and Venezuela significantly complicated their situations by allowing the real values of their currencies to rise. The role of overvalued currencies in inducing capital flight from Argentina, Mexico, and Venezuela is particularly noteworthy. The effect of high real interest rates on savings appears to have been swamped by the effects of exchange rates and the lack of confidence. Only in Mexico does there appear to be a strong correlation between rising real interest rates and increasing savings rates.

Although mistakes in fiscal, exchange rate, and savings policies appear as important proximate causes of the internal shocks that struck Latin America, domestic inflation seems to have been the ultimate cause of these shocks. Most countries were unwilling or unable to adjust nominal exchange rates quickly enough to correct for high and variable rates of inflation, which led to the rise in the real exchange rate value of Latin American currencies. Public sector deficits might in part have been caused by a tendency for the real subsidies on essential goods to rise when the rate of price increases on those goods was kept below the rate of inflation. Finally, attempts to keep domestic interest rates lower than inflation rates restricted the domestic supply of investment funds and forced borrowers to rely even more on overseas sources of funds. It would seem difficult, therefore, to

38. The calculation of the composite swing in public sector deficits uses 1978 and 1982 GDP, expressed in dollars, to construct the averages. Public sector deficits are shown in appendix table B-5, external shock data in table 3. The construction of dollar figures for GDP is detailed in the section on data sources in appendix A.

correct the mistakes in fiscal, exchange rate, and savings policies without attacking the problem of inflation.

### Lender-Borrower Relations

The perceptions of lending institutions also played an important part in the economic crises experienced by these countries.[39] For nearly all the 1970s, Latin American nations kept their debts well below the exposure limits they felt banks would tolerate, although it is unlikely that such limits were ever defined. Countries could thus regularly borrow, even to build up reserves. Although interest rate spreads increased and the average maturity of loans shortened immediately after the oil shock, subsequent trends were positive. In this atmosphere, ordinary economic calculation weakened. Governments let their deficits soar while exercising no effective control on public sector investment. Substantial waste or misallocation undoubtedly occurred.

Signs of stress began appearing in the second half of 1981. By the second half of 1982, following the suspension of principal payments by Mexico, the perception that there was a general Latin American debt problem became prevalent in the financial community. Bank lending to the seven countries had grown at a 28.7 percent annual rate from 1978 to 1981, but it grew only 10.3 percent in 1982 (table 7). This slowdown led to payments problems in a number of the countries. The situation was especially serious in Brazil, where withdrawals of foreign deposits from local banks and the failure to roll over old debts as they came due triggered the eventual suspension of principal payments.

If lender behavior determined the timing of the crisis, the borrowers' own behavior contributed to their vulnerability. Ideally a country should try to match the maturity of its borrowings to the maturity of the items being funded. Thus short-term trade finance should be used for trade, while medium- or long-term loans should be used for projects, which often take years to generate revenues. Furthermore, bank loans should not be used to finance long-term investments, such as hydroelectric plants or mining projects, which often have construction times that exceed the maximum term available on bank loans. But long-term bonds usually appeared too expensive to all these governments, and they used short- and medium-term bank loans to finance investments. In doing so they took the chance that the

39. For a more complete discussion of the relationships between banks and borrowers, see Dale and Mattione, *Managing Global Debt*, pp. 15–25.

31

Table 7. Amount and Maturity Distribution of Bank Loans Outstanding for Seven Latin American Countries, 1977–82

| Country | Loans outstanding (billions of dollars) | | | | Short-term loans[a] (percentage of total loans outstanding) | | | |
|---|---|---|---|---|---|---|---|---|
| | 1977 | 1979 | 1981 | 1982 | 1977 | 1979 | 1981 | 1982 |
| All developing countries | 127.7 | 235.6 | 326.7 | 361.9 | 48.1 | 46.3 | 49.8 | 49.4 |
| Seven Latin American countries | 66.0[b] | 115.9[b] | 181.1[b] | 199.8[b] | 42.6 | 41.1 | 45.9 | 45.8 |
| Argentina | 4.9 | 13.4 | 24.8 | 25.7 | 57.4 | 51.7 | 46.5 | 54.3 |
| Brazil | 25.0 | 38.6 | 52.5 | 60.5 | 31.5 | 29.2 | 34.7 | 34.9 |
| Chile | 1.6 | 4.9 | 10.5 | 11.6 | 60.7 | 40.7 | 39.5 | 39.6 |
| Colombia | 1.8 | 3.6 | 5.4 | 6.3 | 58.9 | 60.8 | 48.7 | 46.1 |
| Mexico | 20.3 | 30.9 | 57.1 | 62.9 | 41.0 | 34.5 | 48.7 | 47.6 |
| Peru | 3.4 | 3.8 | 4.4 | 5.4 | 47.7 | 50.5 | 60.4 | 59.2 |
| Venezuela | 9.1 | 20.8 | 26.2 | 27.5 | 60.6 | 60.9 | 61.4 | 57.5 |

Source: Bank for International Settlements, *Maturity Distribution of International Bank Lending* (Basle: BIS, July 1978, July 1980, July 1982, December 1983).
Note: All figures are for end of year.
a. Up to one year until maturity.
b. Figures may not add because of rounding.

lenders might not roll over loans when they came due, notwithstanding the long-term prospects of a particular project.

Table 7 shows that almost all developing countries have relied heavily on short-term loans. Admittedly, Latin American borrowers as a group show a slightly lower share of short-term loans as a percentage of total bank loans than do other developing nations. But Latin American nations also ran up much higher levels of debt in relation to exports than did other developing nations.[40] Among the seven major Latin American debtors only Brazil has consistently emphasized medium-term loans in its borrowing program. Colombia and Chile considerably improved the maturity structure of their borrowing between 1977 and 1982, but in Chile the action was insufficient to counter the huge buildup in total debt. Peru, Mexico, and Venezuela pursued the worst strategies, with an increasing use of shorter maturities during a rapid buildup in total bank debt. The high ratios of debt to exports made individual nations more susceptible to a payments crisis. But if those countries had been willing to pay the higher spreads necessary for long-term funds, a synchronized crisis of the kind that occurred might not have taken place.

Thus the crisis was caused by three factors: overly expansive and concessive internal policies, external shocks, and improperly structured relations between lenders and borrowers. The question now is: what will it take to overcome the crisis?

## Restoring Growth and Improving Debt-Servicing Capability

Over the past year, responses to the problems of Latin American borrowers have assumed a common pattern that includes rescheduling commercial bank debts, offering new loans prorated on the basis of a bank's existing exposure, and providing IMF loans in exchange for approved stabilization programs. These actions are premised on the hope that in a few years Western economic recovery and better domestic policies in Latin

40. A recent study by Morgan Guaranty Trust suggested that a debt-exports ratio higher than 200 percent is excessive. Argentina, Brazil, Chile, and Mexico had ratios between 253 percent and 388 percent according to that study, while only one other nation (Morocco at 257 percent) among the twenty-one major developing country borrowers had a ratio in that range. Only one Asian nation (the Philippines) even exceeded the 200 percent standard. See "Global Debt: Assessment and Long-Term Strategy," in Morgan Guaranty Trust, *World Financial Markets* (June 1983), pp. 1–15.

America will have restored the healthiness of the debtors. The discussion that follows compares the advantages and disadvantages of the reschedulings and stabilization plans with some other possible solutions to the twin problems of debt and growth in Latin America. The alternative scenarios cover the years 1983 to 1987 for Argentina, Brazil, Chile, Colombia, Mexico, Peru, and Venezuela, which together accounted for about 90 percent of Latin America's debt and output at the end of 1982.

The first section presents the likely consequences of current methods for dealing with the crisis. The second considers the sensitivity of these base-case projections to external economic conditions. Next the possibilities of an investment-led recovery or an export-led recovery are evaluated. This section also provides some information on the trade-off between additional external financing and growth for Latin America under the external economic environment most likely to occur.

None of these scenarios promises to restore economic performance comparable to that of the 1970s. For this reason more radical changes in debtor-creditor relationships cannot be ruled out. The fourth section considers the possibility of restructuring current debts into new loans with reduced interest payments and longer maturities on the assumption that no further funds will be available. The final section looks at the probable results of debt repudiation.

These forecasts are based on models maintained by Data Resources, Inc. (DRI) for seven Latin American economies. Quarterly models are available for Argentina, Colombia, Mexico, Peru, and Venezuela and annual models for Brazil and Chile.[41] It is possible to calculate the sensitivity of the base-case calculations to internal policies and external conditions by changing the inputs to the DRI models. The solution procedure of the models was designed as much as possible to work first with real variables (such as real investment, real exchange rates, and real consumption) in the country models and then to convert into nominal pesos, cruzeiros, sols, and bolivars. It was hoped that this would make the results less susceptible to assumptions about the inflation process, which is difficult to model in these countries.

41. Except in the case of Brazil, the calculations were based on the second quarter 1983 versions of the models, which were updated in May 1983. The Brazilian model was constructed by DRI in July 1983. Some variables vary slightly between the DRI version and the base-case assumptions explained later in this discussion. For example, in the case of Peru the DRI version only includes debt with a maturity greater than one year, while the base case includes all foreign debt.

## Base-Case Projections

Table 8 summarizes the projected external conditions affecting the base case.[42] Economic growth in the West would be moderate but sustained. Interest rates would stay relatively high. Real oil prices would continue to fall through 1984 but would begin recovering in 1985.

The base-case projections assume that in the early years domestic spending and credit policies will reflect IMF stabilization programs for the five countries (Argentina, Brazil, Chile, Mexico, and Peru) already under such programs.[43] In all years Brazil, Chile, Mexico, and Peru are assumed to restrain monetary and fiscal policies to levels implied by the availability of incremental external financing, while Argentina is assumed to make small net repayments of principal in later years because of improvements in the domestic economy. Venezuela has avoided an IMF program so far but has been forced to implement a shadow austerity program of devaluations, reduced spending, and import controls to avoid the IMF's reach in 1983. Venezuelan policies for 1984 to 1987 are assumed to be constrained by the availability of external financing and the need for austerity; an IMF-approved plan probably would not affect the calculations a great deal. Finally, Colombia is assumed to be able to follow easier fiscal and monetary policies to get out of recession, aided by its relatively unconstrained access to external credit.

Prospects for the countries are evaluated on the basis of three criteria: real GDP growth, improvements in debt-exports ratios, and current account performance. Growth serves in this case as a proxy for national welfare. The debt-exports ratio and current account performance indicate the sustainability of foreign financing for a given scenario in the sense that a worsening performance on either of these measures would make countries seem more risky and thereby increase the pressure on lenders to cut back on loans.[44]

42. Further details are in Data Resources, Inc., *Latin American Review, Second Quarter 1983* (Lexington, Mass.: DRI, 1983).

43. Argentina and Chile are operating under standby arrangements with the IMF; Brazil, Mexico, and Peru are working under extended arrangements. See "Transfers of SDRs Amount to SDR 5.2 Billion During Six-Month Period, January–June 1983," *IMF Survey* (August 22, 1983), p. 244. The alternative projections in this study, however, do not assume that countries will meet all their targets, in particular their inflation targets.

44. It is difficult to define whether a country is solvent or able to pay its debts because that is a matter both of politics and economics. For this reason it seems that a country's ability to continue attracting the necessary foreign capital, reflected in improvements in some of the common technical indicators of debt-servicing capacity, is a more useful concept.

35

Table 8. *Projected External Economic Conditions for the Base Case,*
*1983–87*

Percent per year unless otherwise specified

| Conditions | 1983 | 1984 | 1985 | 1986 | 1987 |
|---|---|---|---|---|---|
| Growth in real GNP, United States | 2.6 | 4.8 | 3.8 | 3.5 | 3.5 |
| Growth in real GDP, four European nations[a] | 1.3 | 3.0 | 3.0 | 2.1 | 2.1 |
| Oil price (dollars per barrel) | 28.6 | 27.5 | 31.0 | 35.0 | 39.0 |
| Eurodollar interest rates | 10.2 | 10.4 | 10.9 | 11.2 | 10.6 |
| Long-term interest rates[b] | 10.2 | 9.4 | 9.3 | 9.4 | 9.1 |
| Commodity prices (index) | 33 | 36 | 40 | 42 | 45 |

Source: Computerized data bank maintained by Data Resources, Inc.
a. West Germany, Great Britain, France, and Italy.
b. Weighted average of long-term bond yields in the United States, Canada, Japan, and Europe.

Against these standards the base-case projections do not look encouraging (table 9). Outstanding debts rise from $283.3 billion at the end of 1982 to $342.9 billion at the end of 1987. The composite (seven-country) debt-exports ratio falls from 291 percent to 252 percent, and current account deficits as a share of exports are halved. On the other hand, real GDP in 1987 is only 5.6 percent higher than in 1982, and only in 1986 does the composite GDP exceed the 1982 level. Finally, the 21.1 percent increase in debt over the five years (an average of 3.9 percent per year) is less than the average rate of interest or of U.S. inflation; in other words the aggregate real debt declines, and most of the interest payments are made out of current earnings rather than borrowings, despite projections of a severe recession.

Composite figures may be somewhat misleading, however; in the base case, three countries seem likely to rebound fairly quickly. Colombia is in the best position; its 1987 GDP is 25.8 percent above the 1982 level, with virtually no change in a relatively low debt-exports ratio and a significant reduction in the current account deficit. Chile's GDP grows by 23.9 percent over the five years, accompanied by a significant improvement in the debt-exports ratio. Argentina could have a five-year increase in GDP of 20.2 percent even as it reduces the nominal level of debt and begins to run a current account surplus. Argentina's projected growth is in fact better than at any time since the mid-1970s.

Two other countries turn in tolerable performances. Venezuela shows a moderate upturn (GDP is 12 percent higher in 1987 than in 1982) as an expected improvement in real oil prices in the mid-1980s gradually eases fiscal constraints. Its debt-exports ratio, though essentially unchanged, remains the lowest among the seven countries. Peru experiences a modest

36

growth of 15.0 percent in real GDP over five years but with little improvement in its high debt-exports ratio. Peru would, in fact, have a debt-exports ratio little better than Brazil's (the worst case) in 1987. In addition, this growth in output barely exceeds population growth.[45]

The performances of Mexico and Brazil explain the low growth rates in the composite forecast. Mexico has a five-year growth of 6.7 percent, accompanied by a small decrease in current account deficits as a share of exports. The debt-exports ratio, however, is virtually unchanged. Furthermore, Mexico will have to wait until 1986 for GDP to exceed the 1982 level. In terms of per capita income, Mexicans will still be worse off in 1987 than in 1982, although per capita growth will be positive by 1986.

Brazil faces a truly bleak situation. Modest growth might be restored by 1986, but the recession is so sharp that GDP in 1987 would still be 4.9 percent below the 1982 level. The debt-exports ratio would have improved considerably over that period (from 391 percent to 293 percent), but Brazil still has the worst position on this measure.

Overall, then, it appears that a moderate recovery could restrict the debt and growth problems to Mexico and Brazil if lenders are willing to increase the nominal amounts of their loans outstanding (albeit with reduced exposures in real terms). Only a few middle-sized countries seem destined for per capita growth rates over the next five years that are high enough and sustained enough to undo the problems of the past few years.[46]

45. The devastating impact of weather conditions on Peru's economy has become clearer since these estimates were prepared in mid-1983. For example, DRI lowered its forecast of Peru's 1987 real GDP by more than 10 percent. This would lower real GDP for the seven-country composite by about 0.3 percent. While similar reductions (of 10 percent and 0.3 percent) might therefore be appropriate in the estimates of Peruvian and seven-country composite real 1987 GDP in all scenarios in this chapter, it seemed unnecessary and impractical to redo them.

46. There are two particular causes of the differences between the results of this study and those reported by the Cline or Morgan Guaranty Trust studies. This study uses models to predict the domestic growth resulting from external and domestic policy constraints, rather than assuming domestic growth of 3.5 percent to 4.5 percent from 1984 to 1986 (as Cline assumes in his study; the Morgan Guaranty Trust study makes assumptions about imports based on unstated assumptions about growth). The models in this study are also less optimistic on elasticities, especially on the elasticity of the volume of non-oil exports to growth in industrial countries. Cline assumes an elasticity of 3.0, based on data for all imports of industrialized countries, though the presence of a negative intercept in that formula means that a 3 percent growth rate in industrial countries yields a 6 percent increase in total non-oil exports from developing countries. In this study, on the other hand, calculations are made using estimates of the elasticity of each country's non-oil export volumes to growth in industrial countries. One country (Venezuela) has an elasticity exceeding 3.0; the corresponding figures for Brazil and Chile are around 2.0, and the figures for the other four countries are considerably lower. The differences between the projections for export volume growth are relatively

37

Table 9. Projected Economic Performance in the Base Case for Seven Latin American Countries, 1982–87

| Country | Foreign debt[a] (billions of dollars) | | GDP growth[b] (percent) | Debt-exports ratio (percent) | | Current account deficit as a share of exports (percent) | |
|---|---|---|---|---|---|---|---|
| | 1982 | 1987 | 1983–87 | 1982 | 1987 | 1982 | 1987 |
| Seven countries | 283.3 | 342.9 | 5.6[c] | 290.9 | 252.3 | 33.5 | 6.5 |
| Argentina | 38.0 | 36.5 | 20.2 | 356.8 | 242.0 | 21.4 | -1.8 |
| Brazil | 89.8 | 107.2 | -4.9 | 390.7 | 292.9 | 69.9 | 8.9 |
| Chile | 17.1 | 23.9 | 23.9 | 346.7 | 244.7 | 48.3 | 10.4 |
| Colombia | 10.1 | 16.8 | 25.8 | 213.3 | 211.9 | 50.2 | 15.3 |
| Mexico | 81.6 | 101.6 | 6.6 | 265.6 | 269.2 | 12.5 | 9.2 |
| Peru | 12.0 | 14.3 | 15.0 | 309.0 | 286.2 | 36.4 | 12.8 |
| Venezuela | 34.7 | 42.5 | 12.0 | 177.8 | 178.9 | 22.1 | -2.0 |

Source: Authors' calculations using DRI models.
a. Figures may not add because of rounding.
b. Difference between 1987 real GDP and 1982 real GDP as a share of 1982 real GDP.
c. Individual country performances are weighted by value of 1982 GDP in 1982 dollars.

*Sensitivity to External Economic Conditions*

This section describes the sensitivity of the base-case calculations to increases and decreases in world demand, interest rates, oil prices, and non-oil commodity prices.[47] The alternative assumptions are

— increased demand in industrial countries, with growth in the seven major industrial countries 1 percentage point higher, relative to the base case, from 1983 to 1987;

— decreased demand in industrial countries, with growth in those countries 1 percentage point lower from 1983 to 1987;

— increased interest rates, with Western interest rates 1 percentage point (100 basis points) higher from 1983 to 1987;

— decreased interest rates, with Western interest rates 1 percentage point (100 basis points) lower from 1983 to 1987;

— increased oil prices, 10 percent higher from 1984 to 1987;

— decreased oil prices, 10 percent lower from 1984 to 1987;

— changes in the terms of trade, with prices of non-oil commodity exports 1 percentage point higher (or lower) from 1983 to 1987.[48]

Table 10 and figure 2 show composite results for the seven countries. All these simulations have been carried out under the assumption that internal economic policies (government spending on consumption and investment, money growth, and real exchange rates) are identical with those of the base-case scenario and that the levels of exports, imports, and debt respond to the changed external conditions.

Under those assumptions, if industrial countries were to grow at a rate 1 percentage point above that assumed in the base case and thus increase their demand for imports, 1987 GDP for these seven countries would be 7.3

---

modest when industrial country growth is around 3 percent a year, but Cline's estimates of export volumes would be noticeably higher if annual rates of industrial country growth exceed 3 percent per year. The lower numbers seem particularly appropriate, given that a small but significant share of Latin American exports goes to other developing countries (especially in Latin America) whose recovery will be slower and later than any Western recovery. For details on the other studies see William R. Cline, *International Debt and the Stability of the World Economy* (Washington, D.C.: Institute for International Economics, 1983), pp. 46–73; and Morgan Guaranty Trust Company of New York, "Global Debt: Assessment and Long-Term Strategy," *World Financial Markets* (June 1983), pp. 8–11.

47. Individual country results are discussed in the next two sections, although only aggregate seven-country results are reported in the tables. Individual country results are available from the authors.

48. The relevant commodities are beef, corn, wheat, and wool in Argentina; a general index for Brazil; copper and other commodities for Chile; coffee in Colombia; coffee, cotton, metals, and shrimp for Mexico; and a commodity price index in Peru. No comparable variable existed in the Venezuelan model.

Table 10. *Sensitivity of Economic Performance to Alternative External Economic Conditions for Seven Latin American Countries, Projected 1983–87*

| Conditions | 1987 foreign debt outstanding (billions of dollars) | Real GDP growth, 1983–87[a] (percent) | 1987 debt-exports ratio (percent) | 1987 current account deficit as a share of exports (percent) |
|---|---|---|---|---|
| Base case | 342.9 | 5.6 | 252.3 | 6.5 |
| Increased industrial-country demand | 327.5 | 7.3 | 228.2 | 1.6 |
| Decreased industrial-country demand | 357.6 | 4.1 | 277.4 | 11.6 |
| Increased interest rates | 355.5 | 4.8 | 260.8 | 8.8 |
| Decreased interest rates | 331.2 | 6.4 | 244.2 | 4.5 |
| Increased oil prices | 334.1 | 6.0 | 237.7 | 4.0 |
| Decreased oil prices | 352.3 | 5.4 | 268.3 | 9.4 |
| Improved terms of trade | 319.8 | 5.7 | 222.9 | 0.6 |
| Worse terms of trade | 363.7 | 5.6 | 281.6 | 12.3 |

Source: Authors' calculations.
Note: The countries are Argentina, Brazil, Chile, Colombia, Mexico, Peru, and Venezuela.
a. Difference between 1987 real GDP and 1982 real GDP as a share of 1982 real GDP. Individual country performances are weighted by value of 1982 GDP in 1982 dollars.

percent above the 1982 level, an improvement of 1.7 percent of 1982 GDP in comparison to the base case. Debt would grow at about three-fourths the rate projected in the base case (15.6 percent versus 21.1 percent), debt-exports ratios would fall even further, and the current account would be close to balance in 1987. Chile and Brazil would improve most relative to the base-case predictions (in terms of growth, debt, and debt-exports ratios), while Argentina and Venezuela would see relatively little improvement. Brazil's real GDP in 1987 would still be less than 1982 GDP, however.

A slower recovery in industrial countries, on the other hand, would result in a composite 1987 GDP only 4.1 percent above the 1982 level, foreign debt 26.2 percent above the 1982 figure, and small improvements in the debt-exports ratio and the balance of payments. Such a prospect would seem unacceptable, especially for Brazil, which would have a 1987 GDP 7.0 percent below that of 1982.

A 1 percent decrease in interest rates (whether in the form of narrowed spreads or a reduction in the short-term Eurodollar rates on which loan rates are based) also promises some modest improvement. The level of real GDP in 1987 would be 6.4 percent higher than in 1982 (0.8 percent higher than the 1987 real GDP in the base case), and the debt-exports ratio would fall somewhat more. Venezuela would benefit most in comparison to its

40

performance in the base case, followed by Mexico and Brazil. This result reflects both the high levels of debt and the large share of commercial bank debt for those countries. Conversely, an increase in interest rates would leave 1987 GDP only 4.8 percent above 1982 GDP for the seven countries and would harm Venezuela, Mexico, and Brazil most.

A 10 percent increase in oil prices relative to the base case would help these nations in the aggregate, but by a very small amount. Debt would decrease (increases in Brazil and Argentina would be more than balanced by sharp decreases in Venezuela and Mexico) and real GDP growth would increase slightly. The net effects of a 10 percent decrease in oil prices would be small and in the opposite direction. It is not clear, however, that financial markets would provide the loans necessary to the losers in either of these cases. If external financing were not available, the composite growth performance under both oil-price assumptions would be worse.

Finally, the effects of changes in the terms of trade for major commodity

Figure 2. *Sensitivity of Economic Performance to External Economic Conditions, Seven Latin American Countries*

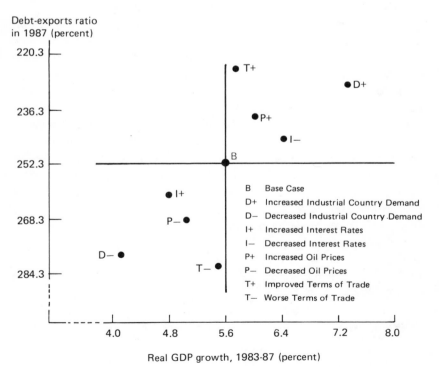

Debt-exports ratio in 1987 (percent)

Real GDP growth, 1983-87 (percent)

B    Base Case
D+   Increased Industrial Country Demand
D−   Decreased Industrial Country Demand
I+    Increased Interest Rates
I−    Decreased Interest Rates
P+   Increased Oil Prices
P−   Decreased Oil Prices
T+   Improved Terms of Trade
T−   Worse Terms of Trade

exports other than oil would be country-specific. In six cases the debt-export ratios would improve following an increase in the non-oil commodity terms of trade, although the effect would be small in Mexico; the model for Venezuela contains no corresponding price variable (almost all of Venezuela's exports are based on petroleum). The effects on growth would be significant in Colombia and Peru but slight in other countries.

### Domestic Policy Options

Latin American nations might also pursue new domestic policies in their attempts to restore growth and to lessen the burden of their foreign debt. This section examines two particular strategies—the implementation of an investment-led recovery (that is, a policy of shifting domestic resources from consumption to investment) and changes in exchange rate policy that would encourage an export-led recovery.

A switch to investment from consumption beyond that implicit in the base case would have very little impact over the next five years (table 11 and figure 3).[49] For the seven countries as a group, growth might even fall slightly, and debt would increase slightly as a consequence of their depressed economic conditions. Because capacity under base-case assumptions is already underutilized, there would be little incentive over the next few years to invest in additional capacity without some signs of future demand for the goods, either foreign demand for exports or domestic demand for consumer goods. In addition, investment in several countries appears to depend more heavily on foreign inputs than do consumer goods, a dependence that further increases debt. Of course, an emphasis on investment would be more appropriate as recovery takes hold. Colombia and Argentina, which are likely to have the strongest recoveries among the seven nations over the next five years, could benefit now from such a policy.

As table 11 and figure 3 show, policies to encourage an export-led recovery seem more promising. This process is best investigated in several stages.[50] If the countries were to devalue their currencies a further 4 per-

49. The following assumptions guided the savings-led recovery scenarios: government spending on consumption is lower by 0.25 percent of base-case GDP, government spending on investment increases by 0.25 percent of base-case GDP, the constant term in the private consumption function is decreased by 0.5 percent of base-case GDP, and the constant term in the private investment function is increased by 0.5 percent of base-case GDP. Base-case GDP was used rather than GDP levels of the alternative scenarios solely for ease in calculation. In the case of Chile, consumption and investment functions are lumped together into a function called the real-gap function in the original model so the shifts have no effect.

50. The export-led recovery projections require a change, relative to the base case, in real exchange rates. Revaluation or devaluation scenarios require a rise or fall, respectively, in the

Table 11. *Sensitivity of Economic Performance to Alternative Domestic Policies for Seven Latin American Countries, Projected 1983–87*

| Policies | 1987 debt (billions of dollars) | Real GDP growth, 1983–1987[a] (percent) | 1987 debt-exports ratio (percent) | 1987 current account deficit as a share of exports (percent) |
|---|---|---|---|---|
| Base case | 342.9 | 5.6 | 252.3 | 6.5 |
| Savings-led recovery | 345.4 | 5.5 | 253.9 | 7.1 |
| Devaluation | 314.6 | 4.3 | 227.9 | −1.8 |
| Revaluation | 372.3 | 7.2 | 277.7 | 15.3 |
| Devaluation with spending adjustments | 340.4 | 13.8 | 245.7 | 5.7 |

Source: Authors' calculations.
Note: The seven countries are Argentina, Brazil, Chile, Colombia, Mexico, Peru, and Venezuela.
a. Difference between 1987 real GDP and 1982 real GDP as a share of 1982 real GDP. Individual country performances are weighted by value of 1982 GDP in 1982 dollars.

cent relative to the base case but hold money growth and government consumption and investment at the levels assumed in the base case, they would see a significant improvement in their debt positions but a small deterioration in their growth rates in relation to their positions in the base case.[51] On the other hand, a revaluation with all other policies held fixed leads to a major deterioration in debt positions but some increase in growth. These simulations may help explain why countries overvalued their currencies during the 1970s, a time when external financing seemed cheap and unconstrained: the buildup in debt can be accompanied by higher growth.

As an alternative, if, after devaluing their currencies, access to credit were maintained at approximately the same level as in the base case, the countries could raise consumption and investment spending, with the resulting implications for imports. They would see a significant increase in GDP in relation to the base case (real GDP would be 13.8 percent higher in 1987 than in 1982, compared to a 5.6 percent improvement in the base case) at the same levels of foreign debt and slightly lower debt-exports ratios. Not only would growth be stronger, but it would return sooner, and

real dollar value of the domestic currency of 2.5 percent in 1984 and 4 percent from 1985 to 1987. For the quarterly models this is represented as a rise or fall, respectively, of 1 percent in the first quarter of 1984 up to 4 percent in the fourth quarter of 1984, which is maintained at 4 percent in all succeeding quarters.

51. The decrease in the debt-exports ratio is due largely to a falling demand for imports in the face of higher import prices. That fall is possible only if total private investment and consumption fall, which in turn decreases GDP growth. Although domestic policies determine the levels of foreign debt in this scenario, it must be remembered that these domestic policies (with the exception of exchange-rate policy) are identical with those in the base case and therefore reflect an austere domestic program.

43

Figure 3. *Sensitivity of Economic Performance to Internal Policies, Seven Latin American Countries*

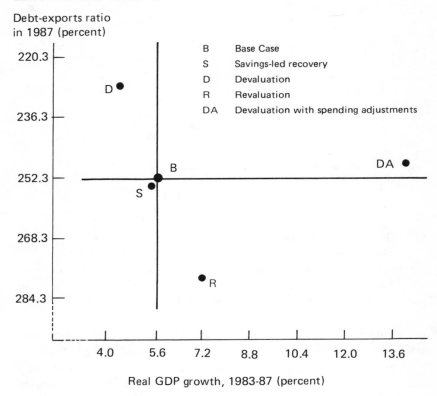

Debt-exports ratio
in 1987 (percent)

Real GDP growth, 1983-87 (percent)

in per capita terms the countries would be as well off in 1987 as in 1982. The effects would be especially strong in Colombia and Brazil, though all countries would benefit some by this strategy.[52] Internally this strategy would result in a shift in favor of the export sector, although the increased growth might be enough to leave everyone better off in absolute terms.

Two elements are indispensable for the success of any attempt at export-led recovery: creditor nations must increase their exposure to debtor countries (approximately 3.7 percent a year in the previous scenarios), and creditor nations must also open their markets and accept the incremental exports from Latin America. The increase in exports from Latin America

52. The effects might not be so strong if countries were to weaken the current measures (tariff and nontariff) that reduce the demand for imports by raising their effective price. While such a liberalization would probably reduce the measured real growth, it should also reduce costs and improve efficiency. These other effects are not measured in the models.

would be matched (in dollar terms, relative to the base case) by an increase in exports to Latin America. The strategy of export-led growth should therefore be palatable to creditor nations.

The calculations from adjusting exchange rates and holding debt each year at the levels of the base case are important for another reason: they provide a forecast of the consequences for growth of allowing Latin American nations to adjust domestic spending in response to changes in the external environment. Thus, in the case of a further 4 percent devaluation, the governments could in effect borrow back $25.8 billion of the foreign exchange they had saved, use those funds to ease domestic austerity programs, and obtain extra output in 1987 equal to 9.5 percent of 1982 GDP—all with a debt level no higher than in the base case (table 11).[53] This implies extra output in 1987 equal to 0.368 percent of 1982 GDP for each $1 billion available to the countries. Although these models are nonlinear, the results still suggest that the cumulative reduction in debt of $11.7 billion relative to the base case following the drop of 100 basis points in interest rates shown in table 10 could perhaps be converted to extra output in 1987 equal to 4.3 percent of the 1982 GDP. Similarly, a stronger recovery in Western demand (annual growth exceeding the base case by 1 percentage point) might be converted into extra 1987 output equal to 5.7 percent of GDP with no increase in debt in relation to the base case. Such calculations hold out the hope that if banks were to continue lending at the rates assumed in the base case, countries could transform both improvements in external circumstances and a greater orientation to the export sector into significant improvements in growth.

## Debt Restructuring: An Alternative?

Debt restructuring is a broad term. For the purposes of this discussion it means schemes that both extend the maturity of the loans and lower interest charges below market rates. Rescheduling, on the other hand, will mean the rollover of existing loans, perhaps accompanied by bank loans on commercial terms. Many restructuring proposals have been made that would allocate the cost of debt restructuring between banks and creditor nations, and various congressmen have made attempts to insert amendments that would have made such conversions a prerequisite for U.S. authorization of funds for the IMF.[54] For the purposes of this discussion a composite debt-

53. This calculation is made by comparing the devaluation scenario with the one assuming devaluation with spending adjustments.

54. The basic features of the best known plans are presented in Dale and Mattione,

restructuring scheme has been used. It has been assumed that all loans outstanding as of December 31, 1982, were consolidated into twenty-two-year loans at a 6 percent interest rate, with two years grace before repayments of principal begin. Furthermore, it has been assumed that no new loans are extended for at least five years after the restructuring. This assumption seems reasonable because commercial banks, the major source of funds for Latin America, would probably be unwilling to make new loans after the value of old loans had been virtually cut in half by such a restructuring.[55]

Such a restructuring would by 1987 make Latin America as a whole worse off than the current reschedulings and stabilization plans (table 12). For the first two years, before repayments of principal begin, debtors would be somewhat better off. Once repayments of principal began, however, the countries would be worse off. Thus after a debt restructuring, GDP in 1987 would be only 3.2 percent higher than in 1982, compared with a 5.6 percent improvement in the base case, even though average GDP during the 1983–87 period under the base case would be slightly lower than with a debt restructuring (the first two years of the base case are very bad). Most of the benefits would accrue to Argentina and Venezuela, although Brazil would also experience a small (and disappearing) improvement during the period. Other countries would experience a great deal of deterioration, however, with Mexico and Peru joining Brazil as countries whose 1987 GDP would actually be below 1982 levels. Other calculations show that the effects would be even worse if no grace period were provided before principal repayments begin.

Of course, the results would be more favorable if net lending were to

*Managing Global Debt*, pp. 42–48. Other loan safeguard plans have also been proposed as an extension of lender-of-last-resort facilities. According to Sumitomo Bank of Japan, at least twenty restructuring and safeguard plans had been proposed as of August 1983; see Charles Smith, "Sumitomo Puts Forward Loan Safeguard Plan," *Financial Times*, August 17, 1983.

55. Banks were earning gross rates of return on Latin American loans of around 13.3 percent in 1983, assuming an average prime interest rate of 11 percent and annualized fees and spreads totaling 2.3 percent. It is necessary, however, to take into account interest costs and other operating expenses for these banks. For the first nine months of 1983 the five largest banks reported figures for annualized net interest income as a share of gross interest-earning assets (domestic and foreign) that ranged between 3.03 percent and 4.42 percent. Among these five banks the highest rate of return on assets after all expenses (including income taxes) was 0.77 percent; the pretax rate of return would probably be two to three times as large. A reduction in spreads to less than 0.5 percent could well make foreign lending unprofitable. Yet most restructuring schemes would lead to very negative spreads; for example, banks would lose 4 to 5 percent per year on their loans to developing countries under Rohatyn's "Worldwide MAC" scheme, described in Dale and Mattione, *Managing Global Debt*. The effective loss in this study's restructuring scenario is also about 4 percent per year.

Table 12. *Economic Performance under Debt Restructurings for Seven Latin American Countries, Projected 1983–87*

Changes in real GDP as a percentage of 1982 GDP

| Country | 1987 GDP | | Average GDP, 1983–87 | |
|---|---|---|---|---|
| | Base case | Restructuring | Base case | Restructuring |
| Seven-country average | 5.6 | 3.2 | 0.2 | 0.6 |
| Argentina | 20.2 | 23.9 | 11.6 | 13.4 |
| Brazil | −4.9 | −4.4 | −6.6 | −5.0 |
| Chile | 23.9 | 9.9 | 12.4 | 0.7 |
| Colombia | 25.8 | 7.5 | 13.0 | 3.2 |
| Mexico | 6.6 | −2.4 | 0.0 | −0.1 |
| Peru | 15.0 | −7.8 | 7.5 | −7.0 |
| Venezuela | 12.0 | 25.4 | 4.5 | 13.2 |

Source: Authors' calculations.

continue despite such a restructuring. This would, however, require substantial commitments from creditor governments, commitments they have been unwilling to make since the mid-to-late 1960s. In light of these considerations, then, the only possible conclusion is that radical restructurings would not improve the situation in Latin America because of the absence of new funds. In fact they might make the situation worse if countries decide it would be better to repudiate their debts because they were already cut off from world capital markets.

### The Possibility of Repudiation.

Western creditors have feared that Latin American debtors might join together to form a debtors' cartel that might even go so far as to repudiate outstanding debts. Although these worries decreased after the September 1983 meeting of the Organization of American States,[56] the possibility of individual or collective actions by debtor nations cannot be rejected out of hand.

The following assumptions underlie an examination of these possibilities. First, debtors repudiate their outstanding debts as of December 31, 1982, and therefore are no longer making interest payments. Second, through one means or another they lose access to any foreign reserves they hold as of that date, but future current account surpluses are used to re-

56. See S. Karene Witcher, "Latin American Nations Pressure Banks But Stop Short of Forming Debtor Cartel," *Wall Street Journal*, September 12, 1983; and William Chislett, "Spectre of Debtors' Club Recedes at Caracas Meeting," *Financial Times*, September 12, 1983.

Table 13. *Economic Performance under Alternative Debt-Repudiation Costs for Seven Latin American Countries, Projected 1983–87*

Changes in real GDP as a percentage of 1982 real GDP

| Country | Base case | | | 5 percent cost of repudiation | | | 10 percent cost of repudiation | | |
|---|---|---|---|---|---|---|---|---|---|
| | 1983 | 1987 | Average | 1983 | 1987 | Average | 1983 | 1987 | Average |
| Argentina | 3.4 | 20.2 | 11.6 | 0.5 | 25.3 | 14.2 | -0.1 | 24.6 | 13.6 |
| Brazil | -5.3 | -4.9 | -6.6 | -5.6[a] | 12.1 | 1.8 | -10.0[b] | 5.0 | -4.9 |
| Chile | 1.1 | 23.9 | 12.4 | -19.9[a] | 18.0 | 3.3 | -24.6[c] | 6.9 | -7.4 |
| Colombia | 2.8 | 25.8 | 13.0 | -4.6[d] | 7.1 | -0.4 | -1.8[e] | 16.9[e] | -0.5[e] |
| Mexico | -4.4 | 6.6 | 0.0 | 2.2[b] | 15.5 | 8.4 | -1.9[b] | -0.4 | -5.7 |
| Peru | 0.0 | 15.0 | 7.5 | -4.9[e] | 7.5[e] | 0.4[e] | -10.8[e] | -7.4[e] | -9.2[e] |
| Venezuela | -1.6 | 12.0 | 4.5 | 2.1[a] | 32.1 | 17.0 | -1.8[b] | 29.1 | 12.0 |

Source: Authors' calculations.
a. Less than two months of reserves in first year.
b. Less than two weeks of reserves in first year.
c. Less than one month of reserves in first year.
d. Negative "reserves" in first year, positive reserves thereafter.
e. Calculations for these cases assume that 1982 reserves are not frozen; if 1982 reserves are frozen, no solution with positive reserves in the 1983–87 period can be obtained. Thus these calculations understate the negative impacts of debt repudiation on Colombia and Peru.

build reserves. Third, in no quarter or year can reserves be negative. Fourth, average reserves in 1987 equal four months of imports to cover any seasonal fluctuations in imports or exports. Fifth, trade in both exports and imports is disrupted, and the costs of disruptions can be modeled by an $X$ percent decrease in unit export earnings and an equivalent percentage increase in unit import costs; these costs are due to foreign suppliers' attempts to insure themselves against new defaults, to creditors' attempts to attach goods and payments, and to the inefficiencies of administering such a scheme. Finally, it is assumed that no new flows of credit are available to Latin America. The nations would then adjust spending upward or downward, depending upon whether the net effect of these new conditions would be to ease or tighten foreign exchange constraints in relation to the base-case scenario.

The results are shown in table 13. It proved impossible to adjust spending in these models so that Colombia or Peru could meet these conditions (in particular, the assumption precluding negative reserves) if the extra cost to trade was 5 percent or more. At the 5 percent level, Chile is also worse off than in the base case, but the solution does satisfy the above conditions. Mexico and Brazil might be better off by 1987, but only if they could survive for the first year with less than one month of reserves. Even if Brazil could survive with one month of reserves, GDP would be lower in the first year after repudiation than could be expected under reschedulings and stabilization plans. Only Argentina and Venezuela might be better off in the medium run and able to build up the necessary reserves in the short run.

If repudiation were to cost 10 percent of export receipts and import revenues, however, the picture changes. Once again, Peru and Colombia could not meet the required conditions. In addition, Chile and Mexico would be much worse off than in the base case and by the end of the first year would have built up less than three weeks of reserves. Brazil might be better off by 1987 by repudiating its debt instead of following current rescheduling and stabilization procedures, although it would suffer even greater hardships in the intervening years. It would only be able to build up ten days of reserves during the first year at the cost of a 10 percent decrease in GDP, almost twice the decrease projected in the base case. Venezuela would find it impossible to build up much more than one week of reserves for the first several years. It would seem, then, that only Argentina could be fairly sure of surmounting a 10 percent cost of repudiation, and at 15 percent even Argentina would be worse off.

These calculations, which do not take into account second-order effects (such as the possibility that reduced trade would lower industrial-country incomes and further diminish demand for Latin American exports), indicate that on economic grounds repudiation is not a better alternative for Latin America than staying with the reschedulings, stabilization plans, and attempts to attract modest amounts of new funds. These economic calculations would be upset if at least some new credits were not made available to Latin America. It is also possible, of course, that more immediate political imperatives could override any consideration of the longer-term economic consequences of repudiation.

## Assessment and Advice

The debt crisis in Latin America is clearly going to last a long time. The combination of a normal world recovery and current stabilization programs might bring the composite debt-exports ratio for the seven major debtors down from 291 percent in 1982 to 252 percent in 1987. This adjustment would be helpful, but in most cases it would probably not be enough to permit restoration of normal market relationships between bankers and borrowers. During these years a sharp break in the growth curve for most of the countries is also expected. Growth may average barely 1.1 percent, far short of earlier performance. Sustained increases in output per capita can be confidently expected only in the second half of the decade, so that growth could be restored to the 3.3 percent level for 1986 and 1987. But if current stabilization programs prove unsustainable, the growth performance and debt-exports ratio may well be even worse.

The picture is not uniformly unfavorable, however. Argentina, Chile, and Colombia could be performing well in 1987, while Peru and Venezuela should have experienced some modest improvements. Yet the difficulties of restoring growth in the two biggest economies, Mexico and Brazil, will continue to threaten progress made elsewhere in Latin America. Furthermore, the chances that frustration and resentment will become ungovernable are not negligible if the crisis is indeed of long duration. Default must therefore be considered a real possibility at some point in the crisis for some countries, despite the absence of economic benefits from such a choice. Such defaults, whether in the extreme form of debt repudiations or the milder form of moratoriums on interest payments, would weaken the U.S. recovery. For example, economists at Data Resources, Incorporated, recently estimated that a moratorium on Brazil's debt would cost the United States $25 billion and 400,000 jobs in 1984, while a moratorium throughout Latin America would raise those figures to $70 billion and 1.1 million jobs.[57]

### Measures for Alleviating the Crisis

The slow process of restoring growth and improving debt-servicing capabilities in Latin America will inevitably be fraught with difficulties. Still, there are ways to help ensure a successful resolution of the situation. An unusually strong and prolonged Western economic recovery would help, as would a decline in world interest rates. The banks have made some concessions by reducing the fees and interest rate spreads charged on several of the refinancings and new credits negotiated during 1984. But it would be unwise to focus all attention on those two factors because there are limits on how much a recovery or a decline in interest rates can do and how quickly those effects would be transmitted to Latin America. That leaves four possible alternatives: additional net lending, trade and exchange rate measures to foster an export-led recovery, policies to bring back flight capital, and debt restructurings.

*Additional net lending.* With constraints as tight as they now appear to be, every additional dollar of resources is valuable. The issue of whether IMF stabilization plans are too austere is often only an issue of whether more capital can be made available. Thus it is necessary to increase IMF resources, to make full use of Inter-American Development Bank and World Bank facilities, and to provide national funds (such as Export-Import Bank loans) on as large a scale as possible.

The increase in IMF resources has been the most crucial link in this process. The adjustment programs already agreed upon have included provision of IMF funds conditioned upon increases in commercial bank loans. This procedure provides considerable leverage to IMF funds while avoiding the danger that they could be used to bail out banks. To sustain this process, however, it was necessary to increase quotas and expand the coverage of the General Arrangements to Borrow in line with the IMF's 1983 proposal. Late in 1983, after nine months of debate, Congress approved the U.S. share of this increase in IMF resources, which totaled about $8.5 billion over five years.[58]

Theoretically, further improvements in growth and debt-servicing capa-

---

57. See "How an LDC Default Would Hit the U.S. Economy," *Business Week* (November 7, 1983), pp. 118, 121.
58. The IMF legislation was contained in H.R. 3959, the Domestic Housing and International Recovery and Financial Stability Act.

bility could be obtained by the mobilization of incremental long-term lending through other multilateral institutions or individual governments. In fact, some efforts have already been made along those lines. The World Bank, for example, made a $400 million loan to Brazil in May 1983, its largest single loan ever to a Latin American country. It also accelerated the disbursements of Brazilian funds and made $800 million (out of a fiscal 1983 total of $1.84 billion) available in the form of a generalized package of financial assistance rather than as project loans.[59] Later in 1983 the United States promised $1.5 billion of new Export-Import Bank credits to Brazil and $500 million to Mexico.[60] But unless some now unforeseen political change permits mobilization of much larger sums, additional lending cannot be relied upon to make more than a marginal contribution to improved debt-servicing capability and higher growth.[61] Still, in such circumstances other official credits can help to strengthen a process that otherwise can lose its credibility all too easily.

*Export-led recovery.* A new and consistent emphasis on the export sector appears to offer Latin American nations substantial potential for restoring growth within given constraints on the level of external debts while at the same time making it possible for industrial countries to expand their own exports to the region. Yet the drawbacks of such a strategy are plain. Not only would it bring higher inflation and lower welfare for the users of imported goods and services, but an export-led recovery will not be feasible unless the governments of Latin America persist in applying the necessary measures over a number of years. In the recent past, many have not been able to achieve such continuity. Nor will an attempt at export-led recovery succeed unless industrial countries accommodate it by importing larger quantities of processed and manufactured goods from Latin America. At a minimum, that implies no new net increases in protective measures applicable to Latin American exports. Still, the much higher market penetration and export orientation of East Asian developing countries suggest that substantial unexploited opportunities remain at current levels of protection.

At the moment, the United States and the developing countries of the Western Hemisphere appear poised to go in opposite directions. The

59. Andrew Whitley, "Brazil Gets $400M Loan from World Bank," *Financial Times*, May 26, 1983.

60. Jonathan Fuerbringer, "$2 Billion More in Latin Loans Backed by U.S.," *New York Times*, August 18, 1983.

61. For example, it would take an estimated $25.8 billion above already expected net borrowings to yield the same improvement in growth from 1983 to 1987 as a cumulative 4 percent real devaluation.

United States has begun to revise its Generalized System of Preferences (GSP) in response to evidence that many of the individual sectors in Latin American and other developing-country economies are modern and highly competitive, although overall income levels have remained low. Current zero-duty entry provisions have in many cases been withdrawn. Meanwhile Latin American countries are adding to their formidable array of protective devices as a means of managing the crisis.

But revision of the GSP authority may present an opportunity to contribute to a solution of the debt crisis. If the U.S. negotiating position were to contain provisions for maintaining or expanding partial or full zero-duty treatment for certain Latin American exports in return for binding cuts in Latin American protection, then negotiation of a new round of tariff and nontariff barrier concessions could be undertaken. Under these conditions the United States would negotiate bilateral deals with Latin American countries only in those products of most interest to the two trading partners. Given the current tariff treatment of Latin American exports (table 14), the large volume of U.S. exports to Latin America ($30.1 billion in 1982), and the sensitivity of Latin American exports to real price changes established earlier, such a bargain could make an important contribution to overcoming the crisis.[62] In addition, cuts in Latin American protection would have the long-term effect of encouraging exports by fostering competitiveness.

Whether or not such a trade bargaining process materializes, Latin American countries should carefully consider the importance of real exchange rates in their attempts to restore growth. Exchange rate policies should be a key item in IMF renegotiation of stabilization programs.

*Flight capital.* Over $37 billion of capital fled the seven countries between 1979 and 1982. If some of those funds could be attracted back, the external financing requirements of Mexico, Argentina, and Venezuela would be reduced. Four prerequisites for the return of this flight capital are good stabilization performance, introduction and maintenance of realistic exchange rates, prospects that rates of return on domestic currency investments will keep pace with inflation, and confidence that the funds will not be confiscated, unduly taxed, or frozen.

It will be especially difficult to meet the last of these conditions because many Latin American nations have recently frozen dollar-denominated accounts or instituted exchange controls in response to their economic difficulties. Nevertheless, as countries move ahead with stabilization plans—

62. Data on exports are from U.S. Department of Commerce, *Survey of Current Business* (June 1983), p. S-17.

Table 14. *U.S. Imports from Seven Latin American Countries, by Import Status, 1982*

Millions of dollars unless otherwise specified

| Country | Total U.S. imports | Status under most-favored-nation clauses | | Status of dutiable goods under General System of Preference | | Free imports under General System of Preference | |
|---|---|---|---|---|---|---|---|
| | | Free | Dutiable | Eligible | Free | As a share of total imports (percent) | As a share of GSP-eligible goods (percent) |
| Argentina | 1,065.8 | 171.2 | 894.5 | 329.1 | 173.2 | 16 | 53 |
| Brazil | 4,171.4 | 1,420.8 | 2,750.6 | 829.6 | 563.9 | 14 | 68 |
| Chile | 668.6 | 223.9 | 444.7 | 391.9 | 150.0 | 22 | 38 |
| Colombia | 799.5 | 494.2 | 305.3 | 154.7 | 63.5 | 8 | 41 |
| Mexico | 15,488.0 | 2,724.7 | 12,763.4 | 2,954.1 | 599.5 | 4 | 20 |
| Peru | 1,072.5 | 377.5 | 695.0 | 136.4 | 104.0 | 10 | 76 |
| Venezuela | 4,757.3 | 281.8 | 4,475.5 | 50.1 | 46.6 | 1 | 93 |

Source: Office of the United States Trade Representative

currently only Mexico's stabilization program might have advanced far enough—they should consider offering a special one-time, no-questions-asked opportunity to return flight capital. Mexico's earlier experiment with Mexdollars provides part of the instrument needed—a facility in which residents and nonresidents could make dollar deposits. The earlier Mexdollar accounts were unsuccessful because the dollar-denominated deposits were used to make peso-denominated loans, which deprived depositors of a safe cover for their deposits and increased expectations that a crisis would lead to a freeze on them. A facility with a separate legal existence that is limited to investing in dollar instruments held by creditor banks on condition that they use the funds for domestic operations might be the answer.

*Debt restructurings.* Complicated formulas for alleviating the debt problem through radical debt restructurings are not likely to succeed. These schemes would cut off access to funds by turning good loans into bad and would force substantial repayments of principal at a time when Latin American countries clearly need to borrow moderate amounts in their attempts to restore growth. Furthermore, the situations of the countries vary enough so that it would be excruciatingly difficult to formulate a single set of terms acceptable to all. It appears more sensible to concentrate on sustaining Western growth, reducing interest rate spreads, and implementing the other policies mentioned previously. Should present reschedulings and stabilization plans prove insufficient, any new solution must not be so severe as to scare away likely providers of future credits.

## Political Dangers

The picture that emerges from this analysis is sobering for both debtors and creditors. Implicit in the politics and provisions of the stabilization programs adopted so far is the expectation that overcoming the crisis will entail a few years of tough adjustments and will then be followed by high levels of growth. That expectation is not supported by the analysis here, particularly in regard to Mexico and Brazil. In the absence of a new boom in commodity prices, which nobody now predicts, the only apparent way to improve the outlook is through measures such as real currency devaluations and export incentives that governments in the past have found either distasteful or impossible. Meanwhile, borrowers, creditors, and the IMF are likely to continue the grinding business of trading continued or renewed stabilization measures for refinancings. It is conceivable that in such a future people will become resigned to low growth as the only available option and that refinancing negotiations will become institutionalized, so that a new normalcy will appear.

Conceivable, but not probable. In most countries, stabilization plans have been sold as a short, necessary operation, soon to result in a new burst of growth. In some they are being instituted by technicians without broad political consent. When the crisis in some countries drags on with per capita incomes below 1980 levels, as they may be for much of this decade, and without credible promise of relief, it is easy to imagine resentment and frustration exploding and turning against governments when they fail to persuade the United States and other industrial countries of the need for more generous terms. Not only would the current broad but weak trend toward democracy falter, but public order and national security could also be at risk. And it is worth remembering that after a generation of often failed national security governments, military intervention may no longer be the plausible alternative it was in the 1960s and 1970s.

No one can accurately predict the degree of danger involved in a prolonged crisis of debt and growth. But it is sufficiently great to justify every effort to manage the crisis through facilitating trade, adjusting exchange rates, promoting capital reforms, and providing additional funds. The alternative could be unrest throughout the hemisphere.

## Appendix A: Calculation Methods and Data Sources

### Calculations of External Shocks

Calculations of the magnitude of external shocks in this study are based on the methods employed by Bela Balassa in analyzing the impact of the first oil shock on developing countries. The calculations here are not as detailed because the data on individual commodities used by Balassa are only available with a long lag. On the other hand, the following calculations try to account for the impact of changing interest rates on the net interest component of the services balance.[63] The years 1976–78 served as the base period in calculating the magnitude of external shocks received from 1979 to 1982. Four categories of shocks are calculated for each country.

63. See Bela Balassa, "The Newly-Industrializing Developing Countries after the Oil Crisis," *Weltwirtschaftliches Archiv*, vol. 117 (1981), pp. 142–94; "Structural Adjustment Policies in Developing Economies," Staff Working Paper 464 (Washington, D.C.: World Bank, July 1981); and "Adjustment to External Shocks in Developing Economies," Staff Working Paper 472 (Washington, D.C.: World Bank, July 1981).

First, the terms-of-trade shock is calculated. This has two parts, one reflecting export price changes, the other import price changes.

The difference between export prices in a given year and base-period export prices corrected for inflation, multiplied by current export volumes, gives the shock caused by export price shifts. This can be written as

$$XS_t = (P_t^X - PB_t^X) \times XVol_t ,$$

where $XS_t$ denotes the export shock in year $t$ measured in current dollars, $P_t^X$ denotes actual export prices in year $t$, $PB_t^X$ denotes the price of exports in the base period corrected for inflation between the base period and year $t$, and $XVol_t$ denotes actual export volumes in year $t$. A positive value for $XS_t$ means that a country was favorably affected in year $t$ by export price movements; a negative value indicates an unfavorable movement.

Similarly, the difference between base-period import prices corrected for inflation and import prices in the given year, multiplied by current import volumes, gives the shock due to import price shifts. This can be written as

$$MS_t = (PB_t^M - P_t^M) \times MVol_t ,$$

where $MS_t$ denotes the import shock in year $t$, measured in current (year $t$) dollars, $PB_t^M$ is the base-period import price corrected for inflation, $P_t^M$ is the current price of imports, and $MVol_t$ is actual import volume in year $t$. A negative value for $MS_t$ means that a country was unfavorably affected by import price changes.

These two shocks can then be combined to yield the total terms-of-trade shock facing a country,

$$TOT_t = XS_t + MS_t ,$$

where $TOT_t$ is the total terms-of-trade shock in year $t$ measured in current dollars.

In light of the importance attached to the oil price shocks of 1979–82 in explanations of Latin America's difficulties, it is useful to calculate that shock separately. For an oil importer, this is

$$OIL_t^M = (PB_t^{Oil} - P_t^{Oil}) \times OVol_t^M ,$$

where $OIL_t^M$ is the current dollar value of the shock, $PB_t^{Oil}$ the base-period oil price corrected for inflation, $P_t^{Oil}$ the actual price of oil in year $t$, and

$OVol_t^M$ the actual oil import volumes. For oil importers, the oil shock $OIL_t^M$ is just one component of the import price shock $MS_t$. The comparable expression for an oil exporter is

$$OIL_t^X = (P_t^{Oil} - PB_t^{Oil}) \times OVol_t^X ,$$

with $OIL_t^X$ the current dollar value of the oil shock for an oil exporter, $PB_t^{Oil}$ and $P_t^{Oil}$ the same as before, and $OVol_t^X$ the actual volume of oil exports. For either $OIL_t^X$ or $OIL_t^M$ a positive value indicates a favorable shock.

These calculations treat current volumes (of total exports, total imports, or oil trade) as if they were chosen regardless of the prices prevailing in international markets. In that sense the calculations may not completely capture the shock facing the country. Thus measures that encourage excessive imports (for example, subsidized domestic oil prices or overvalued exchange rates) would lead to an overstatement of the shock due to import price increases in relation to the base period, while a country that adjusted imports rapidly in response to relative price changes might have its shock underestimated. Similarly, it should be noted that these calculations imply that Latin American nations cannot influence the prices prevailing in their export and import markets. This would appear to be true in all markets except the export markets for coffee and (perhaps) oil.

Finally, these calculations assume that the marginal cost of supplying current volumes of exports is less than the inflation-adjusted base-period price of exports for all quantities between zero and the actual volume in a given year. If the marginal cost of supplying current volumes of exports exceeds the inflation-adjusted base price, however, then the calculated shock ideally would be reduced by the amounts of excess costs incurred in attaining that volume of exports. These calculations capture those excess production costs only if they led to an increase in import costs. This consideration is probably most relevant in the case of Mexico's oil production, which was expanding rapidly during the period. The calculation of the oil shock component for Mexico does not include any induced increases in import prices, although the total terms-of-trade shock for Mexico does include that effect.

Next the effects of Western recession on the demand for Latin America's non-oil exports is calculated. This shock is defined as

$$DEM_t = XVolB \times PB_t^X \times (GR_t - GRB_t),$$

where $DEM_t$ is the demand shock measured in current dollars, $XVolB$ is the volume of non-oil exports in the base period, $GR_t$ is the actual growth in trade to year $t$, and $GRB_t$ is the cumulative growth in world trade volumes that would have occurred if the 1976–78 average rate of expansion had continued to year $t$. A positive value of $DEM_t$, which is obtained when cumulative actual growth exceeds "normal" growth, denotes a favorable shock. Oil exports are excluded from the calculation because a significant part of the volume shortfalls were caused by conscious decisions of oil producers. This demand-shock calculation is based on the assumption that countries would hold their base-period share in world markets whatever the level of total world trade.

The effects of high real interest rates on countries are defined as

$$INT_t = (RR_B - RR_t) \times DEBT_{t-1},$$

where $DEBT_{t-1}$ equals outstanding debt at the end of the previous year (equivalently, at the beginning of the current year), $RR_t$ denotes the real interest rate in the current year (that is, the difference between nominal interest rates and the inflation rate in the current year), $RR_B$ denotes the real interest rate in the base period, and $INT_t$ is the measured interest rate shock. A negative number denotes an unfavorable shock. This calculation only takes into account the market level of interest rates on Eurodollar deposits; it does not correct for changes in the spreads, or risk premiums, that borrowers have paid. Spreads for all LDC borrowers averaged 1.49 percent from 1976 to 1978 and fell in 1979.[64] It appears that until 1982, spreads rarely exceeded this base-period level. Thus a recalculation including spreads would probably reduce the calculated interest rate shocks for 1979 to 1981, and would increase the amounts for 1982 by the equivalent of one percentage point. The cumulative figures are unlikely to vary much.

This method of calculation assigns external shocks to a category determined by the proximate cause of the shock, not the ultimate cause. In particular, high real interest rates had a direct effect on countries through higher interest costs on old debts and indirect effects through the slowdown in world trade and the fall in commodity prices. Only the direct effect is defined as an interest rate shock in these calculations. The indirect effects are included as demand shocks and terms-of-trade shocks, respectively.

In several places specific assumptions have been made to facilitate computation. First of all, the interest rate shock, $INT_t$, is calculated only on bank debt outstanding. This avoids the need to make assumptions about the magnitude of short-term suppliers' credits for all countries and of medium-

64. World Bank, *World Development Report, 1980* (Washington, D.C.: World Bank, 1980), p. 27.

term nonbank loans to private borrowers not covered by official guarantees in countries not reporting such data. It also avoids the need to make assumptions about the financing terms applicable to nonbank debt. Anyway, in most cases bank loans are the major source of debt outstanding and the item most affected by changing interest rates.

Furthermore, in the cases of Colombia and Chile it is necessary to make assumptions about the volume of oil imports, which are not reported for all years. For Chile, data were available only until 1978; it was therefore assumed that oil import volumes held steady at base-period levels through 1982. Data on Colombia's oil imports were available until 1980; it was assumed that oil import volumes held steady in 1981 and 1982 at 1980 levels.

### Calculation of Inflation-Adjusted Current Accounts

The shocks that a country faces must be compared with the deterioration in the current account to get some measure of a country's adjustment position. These figures must also be adjusted for inflation in a way that is compatible with the external shock calculations.

For this purpose the current account balance is divided into two parts: the first consists of net interest payments and net earnings on foreign direct investment; the second is the nonfinancial current balance. This can be written as

$$CA = NCB - NI,$$

where $CA$ is the current account balance, $NI$ represents net payments of interest and dividends, and $NCB$ includes all other current payments. The 1976–78 period is used to construct normal net positions for these two items, denoted $NCB_B$ and $NI_B$. The normal position of the non-interest portion in future years is then

$$NCB_t^N = NCB_B \times PI_t,$$

where $PI_t$ is the price level in year $t$, and $PI$ in the base period equals 1.0. The normal position for the net interest portion is

$$NI_t^N = NI_B \times (\Delta PI_t + RR_B)/R_B,$$

where $\Delta PI_t$ is the inflation rate in year $t$, $RR_B$ is the real interest rate in the base period, and $R_B$ is the nominal interest rate in the base period. Since $R_B = \Delta PI_B + RR_B$, where $\Delta PI_B$ is the inflation rate in the base period, it can be seen that $NI_t^N$ gives the net interest position that would have resulted if nominal interest rates had increased only as much as inflation. Then the normal inflation-adjusted current account position in year $t$ would be

$$CA_t^N = NCB_t^N - NI_t^N .$$

The deterioration in the current accounts, CAD, is then defined as

$$CAD_t = CA_t - CA_t^N ,$$

where $CA_t$ is the actual current account balance. A positive number for $CAD_t$ implies that the current account position deteriorated less (or improved more) than expected after accounting for inflation only. If $CAD_t$ is greater than the total external shock experienced, that is,

$$CAD_t > TOT_t + INT_t + DEM_t ,$$

then the country has adjusted policies so as to diminish (increase) the unfavorable (favorable) impact of the external shocks on the balance of payments. If

$$CAD_t < TOT_t + INT_t + DEM_t ,$$

the country has changed policies so as to increase (use up) the unfavorable (favorable) impact of external shocks.

### Data Sources

Inflation figures were derived from the GNP implicit price deflator for the United States, available in the *Economic Report of the President*. Calculation of shocks caused by export price shifts required data on export volumes, export prices, and inflation. Export volumes were constructed from data on revenues from exports of goods (in the IMF's *International Financial Statistics*, hereafter *IFS*) and export prices (*IFS* data for Brazil and Colombia; Data Resources, Inc., data for the other five nations).

Calculation of shocks due to import price shifts required data on import volumes, inflation, and import prices. Import price data are from *IFS* data (Brazil and Colombia) and DRI (other five). Import volumes were constructed from *IFS* data for expenditures on imports of goods (FOB basis) and above-mentioned data on prices.

Oil shocks were also calculated from revenue and price data. Oil price data came from the United Nations *Monthly Statistical Bulletin.* Oil revenues (or expenditures) came from *IFS* data (for Argentina, Brazil, Mexico, Peru, and Venezuela). Some annual data were unavailable for Chile and Colombia, so data from the *IFS Trade Supplement* were used along with *IFS* data on total imports of goods to construct oil import volumes for Colombia and Chile.

Calculation of demand shocks required data on inflation (*IFS*), export revenues (*IFS*), and growth in world trade. Data on growth in world trade came from the IMF *Annual Report* for 1983.

Interest rate shocks were calculated using inflation data (*IFS*), Euro-dollar deposit rates (*IFS*), and outstanding loans from banks (Bank for International Settlements, *Maturity Distribution of International Bank Lending).*

The GDP figures necessary for table 3 were converted into dollars using yearly-average exchange rates (*IFS*). The domestic currency GDP figures for 1979 to 1981 in all countries, and for Chile, Mexico, and Venezuela in 1982, are *IFS* data; 1982 GDP data for the other countries came from the DRI models. Because there is a significant discrepancy between DRI and *IFS* figures for Argentina from 1979 to 1981, the 1982 GDP figure from DRI was adjusted upwards by the average discrepancy (in percentage terms) prevailing from 1979 to 1981.

Calculations of deterioration in the current account balance required data on current account deficits and interest payments from the IMF's *Balance of Payments Statistics Yearbook* (*BOP*).

Capital flight estimates for 1979 to 1982 are the sum of the "net errors and omissions" and "other short-term capital, other sectors" entries in *BOP*. The latter entry excludes banks and the government sector.

*Bibliography of Data Sources*

Bank for International Settlements. *Maturity Distribution of International Lending.* Basle: BIS, various releases, July 1979, July 1980, July 1981, July 1982.

Data Resources, Inc. Latin American models, second quarter 1982. (These data were obtained from a computerized data bank, not a published source. They are based on figures published by the IMF and by government agencies in the various countries.)

*Economic Report of the President, February 1983*, p. 166.

International Monetary Fund. *Annual Report: 1983.* Washington, D.C.: IMF, 1983, p. 19.

International Monetary Fund. *Balance of Payments Statistics, 1983 Year-book*, vol. 34, pt. 1. Washington, D.C.: IMF, 1983.

International Monetary Fund. *International Financial Statistics*, vol. 36 (July 1983).

International Monetary Fund. *International Financial Statistics, 1983 Yearbook*. Washington, D.C.: IMF, 1983.

International Monetary Fund. *International Financial Statistics: Supplement on Trade Statistics, 1983*. Washington, D.C.: IMF, 1983.

United Nations. *Monthly Statistical Bulletin*, vol. 38 (September 1983), p. 184.

## Appendix B: Supplementary Tables

This appendix contains tables presenting data on savings and investment rates, public sector deficits, real exchange rates, and inflation in the seven major Latin American countries. These data are used in the section "Country Patterns," which analyzes individual domestic policies of the countries in detail.

Table B-1. *Investment in Latin America, 1978–82*

Percentage of GDP

| Country | 1978 | 1979 | 1980 | 1981 | 1982[a] |
|---------|------|------|------|------|------|
| Argentina | 24.8 | 24.1 | 25.7 | 22.0 | 17.1 |
| Brazil | 20.8 | 19.8 | 21.1 | 19.2 | 19.1 |
| Chile | 17.8 | 17.8 | 20.7 | 22.0 | 16.5 |
| Colombia | 18.2 | 18.1 | 19.0 | 20.0 | 19.5 |
| Mexico | 23.6 | 26.0 | 28.1 | 29.0 | 20.9 |
| Peru | 14.6 | 14.6 | 17.7 | 21.3 | 21.0 |
| Venezuela | 42.6 | 31.9 | 24.3 | 23.4 | 26.4 |

Source: Unpublished Department of State data.
Note: All figures include changes in stocks.
a. Figures for 1982 are preliminary estimates.

## Table B-2. *Private Investment in Latin America, 1978–82*

Percentage of GDP

| Country | 1978 | 1979 | 1980 | 1981 | 1982[a] |
|---------|------|------|------|------|---------|
| Argentina | 11.8 | 13.3 | 15.6 | 11.1 | 8.0 |
| Chile | 11.1 | 12.7 | 15.6 | 16.7 | n.a. |
| Colombia[b] | 9.8 | 10.0 | 9.8 | 10.0 | 9.4 |
| Mexico | 16.4 | 18.1 | 18.6 | 16.1 | 10.6 |
| Peru | 9.0 | 9.3 | 10.3 | 13.1 | 15.0 |
| Venezuela[b] | 24.3 | 18.7 | 11.4 | 8.9 | 7.9 |

Source: Unpublished Department of State data.
n.a. Not available
Note: Data include changes in stocks unless otherwise noted.
a. Figures for 1982 are preliminary estimates.
b. Private investment figures for Colombia and Venezuela exclude changes in stocks.


## Table B-3. *Savings in Latin America, 1978–82*

Percentage of GDP

| Country | 1978 | 1979 | 1980 | 1981 | 1982[a] |
|---------|------|------|------|------|---------|
| Argentina | 27.8 | 23.6 | 22.6 | 17.9 | 12.7 |
| Brazil | 17.4 | 15.2 | 15.9 | 15.3 | 14.5 |
| Chile | 10.7 | 12.1 | 13.5 | 7.4 | n.a. |
| Colombia | 19.9 | 20.1 | 19.4 | 15.5 | 13.8 |
| Mexico | 20.5 | 21.8 | 24.1 | 23.2 | 19.2 |
| Peru | 12.8 | 19.9 | 18.0 | 13.8 | 17.0 |
| Venezuela | 29.6 | 33.9 | 32.5 | 29.2 | 24.1 |

Source: Unpublished Department of State data.
n.a. Not available.
a. Figures for 1982 are preliminary estimates.


## Table B-4. *Private Savings in Latin America, 1978–82*

Percentage of GDP

| Country | 1978 | 1979 | 1980 | 1981 | 1982[a] |
|---------|------|------|------|------|---------|
| Argentina | 21.7 | 20.0 | 21.0 | 21.3 | 17.8 |
| Chile | 2.0 | 2.9 | 2.7 | 1.5 | n.a. |
| Colombia | 13.3 | 12.7 | 12.4 | 9.4 | 9.4 |
| Mexico | 17.3 | 18.8 | 22.0 | 24.1 | 25.6 |
| Peru | 13.4 | 15.6 | 16.0 | 13.4 | 12.8 |
| Venezuela | 15.8 | 16.0 | 12.8 | 15.0 | n.a. |

Source: Unpublished Department of State data.
n.a. Not available.
a. Figures for 1982 are preliminary estimates.

Table B-5. *Consolidated Public Sector Deficits in Latin America, 1978–82*

Percentage of GDP

| Country | 1978 | 1979 | 1980 | 1981 | 1982a |
|---------|------|------|------|------|-------|
| Argentina | 6.9 | 7.2 | 8.6 | 14.3 | 14.2 |
| Brazil | 6.1 | 8.1 | 7.1 | 12.1 | 13.8 |
| Chile | −2.1 | −4.8 | −5.6 | −1.1 | 4.0 |
| Colombia | 1.1 | 1.2 | 2.5 | 3.6 | 5.8 |
| Mexico | 5.7 | 6.8 | 7.7 | 14.8 | 18.6 |
| Peru | 6.3 | 1.7 | 6.4 | 8.6 | 8.8 |
| Venezuela | 10.4 | −1.1 | −1.2 | 3.4 | 11.0 |

Source: Unpublished Department of State data.
Note: Includes interest payments.
a. Figures for 1982 are preliminary estimates.


Table B-6. *State Enterprise Deficits in Latin America, 1978–82*

Percentage of GDP

| Country | 1978 | 1979 | 1980 | 1981 | 1982a |
|---------|------|------|------|------|-------|
| Argentinab | 2.0 | 2.9 | 3.1 | 3.7 | 5.4 |
| Brazil | n.a. | n.a. | 3.4 | 4.2 | 5.0 |
| Chile | 0.1 | 0.4 | 0.0 | 1.8 | 1.6 |
| Colombia | 1.8 | 0.8 | 1.4 | 1.6 | 2.4 |
| Mexico | 2.8 | 3.5 | 4.6 | 8.0 | 8.6 |
| Peru | 1.2 | 1.1 | 3.5 | 3.7 | 4.9 |
| Venezuela | 6.3 | 1.4 | −1.4 | 5.2 | 8.3 |

Source: Unpublished Department of State data.
Note: State enterprise deficits in Chile, Colombia, Peru, and Venezuela equal consolidated public sector deficits minus central government deficits; in Mexico the state enterprise deficit equals consolidated public sector deficit minus the federal government deficit.
a. Figures for 1982 are preliminary estimates.
b. Figures for Argentina include interest payments.


Table B-7. *Inflation in Latin America, 1978–82*

Percent per year

| Country | 1978 | 1979 | 1980 | 1981 | 1982 |
|---------|------|------|------|------|------|
| Argentina | 175.3 | 159.6 | 100.8 | 104.5 | 164.8 |
| Brazil | 38.7 | 52.7 | 82.8 | 105.6 | 98.0 |
| Chile | 40.1 | 33.4 | 35.1 | 19.7 | 9.9 |
| Colombia | 17.8 | 24.7 | 26.5 | 27.5 | 24.6 |
| Mexico | 17.5 | 18.2 | 26.4 | 27.9 | 58.9 |
| Peru | 57.9 | 66.7 | 59.2 | 75.4 | 64.4 |
| Venezuela | 7.0 | 12.4 | 21.5 | 16.2 | 9.9 |

Source: Constructed from consumer price indexes in IMF, *International Financial Statistics, 1983 Yearbook* (Washington, D.C.: IMF, 1983).

## Table B-8. *Real Exchange Rates in Latin America, 1978–82*

Constant domestic currency units per constant dollar

| Country | 1978 | 1979 | 1980 | 1981 | 1982 |
|---|---|---|---|---|---|
| Argentina | 96.1 | 69.3 | 60.2 | 75.4 | 132.0 |
| Brazil | 99.3 | 103.2 | 106.9 | 99.3 | 105.6 |
| Chile[a] | 104.1 | 88.0 | 72.0 | 71.5 | 93.0 |
| Colombia | 93.9 | 86.9 | 85.0 | 86.4 | 85.7 |
| Mexico | 100.5 | 92.5 | 81.7 | 76.8 | 116.9 |
| Peru[b] | 120.4 | 112.7 | 99.4 | 90.9 | 96.7 |
| Venezuela[c] | 97.9 | 96.4 | 85.7 | 81.5 | 79.6 |

Methods and sources: Each country's real exchange rate was indexed to an average 1976–78 value of 100. The GNP deflator was used for the U.S. price index; the wholesale price index was used for domestic prices in Latin America, except as noted. For data on exchange rates and Latin American prices, see IMF, *International Financial Statistics, 1983 Yearbook;* for U.S. GNP deflator data, see *Economic Report of the President, February 1983,* p. 166.

a. Home goods price index used for Chile.
b. Consumer price index used for Peru.
c. Home goods price index used for Venezuela.